# PREMINGER

# PREMINGER

An Autobiography

by

OTTO PREMINGER

Doubleday & Company, Inc.
Garden City, New York
1977

Library of Congress Cataloging in Publication Data

Preminger, Otto.
    Preminger.

    Includes index.
    1. Preminger, Otto.   2. Moving-picture producers and
directors—United States—Biography.
PN1998.A3P672 1977      791.43'023'0924 [B]
ISBN: 0-385-03480-6
Library of Congress Catalog Card Number: 74-18825

# CONTENTS

# PREMINGER

# I

## MY SECOND BIRTHDAY

The twenty-first of October, 1935, was my second birthday. Not the kind with two candles on the cake. In fact I was almost twenty-nine years old and was standing on deck of the French liner *Normandie* watching the Statue of Liberty come closer and closer and beyond her—for the first time—the skyline of New York. I was so overcome with emotion that I could not control my tears. I was swept by the feeling that a new life was beginning. The Otto Preminger whose address had been Vienna was finished. The American Otto Preminger was starting.

All the circumstances that brought me here had the quality of dream-wish fulfillment. It began in Vienna about six months earlier. One of Hollywood's most powerful men, Joseph M. Schenck, arrived on a visit to his old friend Julius Steger, who, after making a fortune in the United States, had returned to his native Vienna. He told Schenck about me, the young man who two years before had succeeded the legendary Max Reinhardt as head of the famous Theater in der Josefstadt. Reinhardt resigned in 1933 from the management of the theatre which he bought in 1924 and renovated splendidly, assisted by the unlimited generosity of Austria's richest man, Camillo Castiglioni.

During the Depression, Castiglioni lost his fortune and the theatre got into a precarious financial situation. By a combination of hard work, intuition, and luck I was able to rescue it from bankruptcy.

One morning in mid-April 1935 I was rehearsing a new intimate musical, *The King with the Umbrella,* when my secretary rushed onto the stage and interrupted the rehearsal to tell me excitedly that Mr. Joseph M. Schenck wished to see me that afternoon at five o'clock at his hotel. I was impressed but I had a schedule to maintain. "Tell Mr. Schenck," I instructed my secretary, "that I will still be rehearsing at five o'clock. I am very sorry." She was aghast and stood glaring at me waiting to see if I would come to my senses, but I continued my rehearsal. Finally she fled, returning a few minutes later, her face beaming. Mr. Schenck would see me at my convenience.

I arrived at his hotel at 10 P.M. Julius Steger greeted me and ushered me into an enormous living room filled with antique furniture in the midst of which three incongruous card tables had been set up. About a dozen men were sitting around them smoking cigars and playing cards in their shirt sleeves. Schenck, a balding man in his late fifties, rose abruptly and led the way into a bedroom followed by me and Steger, who acted as our interpreter since I spoke no English and Schenck no German. He closed the door and explained that about a year ago he had bought the gigantic Fox corporation and merged it with his independent film company, Twentieth Century. He and his partner, Darryl Zanuck, to whom he referred several times as a genius, had most ambitious plans for their new company and were looking for creative young people. He said that I had the right qualifications and I discovered that he had investigated my background thoroughly. He knew that I had started as an actor in Reinhardt's illustrious ensemble when I was just seventeen, switched to directing at nineteen, and at twenty-five had taken over Reinhardt's theatre. He was not in the least concerned that I spoke no English and had directed only one small, entirely forgettable film. Those details did not trouble me either and I agreed on the spot to wind up my affairs in Vienna and leave for Hollywood. I was to cable him as soon as I was ready and he would arrange my passage. He did not mention a contract or money, nor did I. We shook hands and he returned to his card game. Steger embraced me and showed me to the door.

My parents were shocked by my decision and so was Camillo Castiglioni, who owned the theatre. They warned me against leaving Vienna, the beautiful city where I had attained success and fame at an early age, where my future was secure, where I was surrounded by a family and friends who adored me. It was madness to leave all this for a country where I was totally unknown, for a land of strangers whose language I did not speak. They implored me to reconsider but I remained firm.

I immediately started to take English lessons from a young American who studied at the University in Vienna.

Gilbert Miller, the Broadway producer who was an intense follower of European theatre and had seen several of my productions, learned in London that I was going to Hollywood at Schenck's expense. He called me and asked if I would stop over in New York and direct his Broadway production of a West End hit *Libel!* a courtroom drama by Edward Wooll. I had produced and directed the German version of the play in Vienna under the title *Sensationsprozess* a few months earlier. I accepted gladly, again without bringing up the question of money.

I sailed for America on the *Normandie*. So did Gilbert Miller and his wife, Kitty. The Millers were addicted to the company of the rich, the famous, and the social. They introduced me to the most elegant of the *Normandie*'s passengers, among them a genuine Maharani, I think of Kapurthala, and a stupendously tall and boring Grand Duke who was on board in order to present a medal to the captain of the *Normandie* for breaking the speed record at her second crossing of the Atlantic.

I soon made an unsettling discovery concerning my English lessons in Vienna. I had progressed to the point where I could understand my tutor and speak to him in what I took to be acceptable English. But I realized on the *Normandie* almost immediately that my self-confidence was misplaced. I could comprehend almost nothing of the conversations around me. No one guessed because I smiled and nodded and used a handful of simple phrases I had memorized.

It struck me that it might be helpful to study the original version of *Libel!* and the German translation side by side. I spent most of my days in my cabin until I could recite the play by heart in both languages.

In the evenings, after the Millers and their social friends retired, I used to descend in the ship's golden elevator to the second class where the passengers had more fun and the women were younger. My companion on these expeditions was Felix Ferry, a multilingual Romanian, raised in Paris and known to everyone as Féfé. He was traveling to New York to hire some long-legged American girls for a night-club revue he was producing at the Dorchester Hotel in London. Féfé was to become for the rest of his life one of my closest friends.

The day I arrived in New York for the first time was auspiciously sunny and warm, the most beautiful weather imaginable. Féfé was met at the pier by his friend Louis Shurr, an actors' agent, and the Millers by Kitty's father, Jules Bache, one of America's wealthiest stockbrokers. We decided to celebrate with lunch at the "21" Club, which was then, as it is now, New York's top restaurant. Our party filled an entire section of the place. One of the owners, Jack Kriendler, offered to show me around. He and his partner, Charles Burns, had started "21" as a speakeasy during Prohibition and following repeal converted it into a legitimate restaurant. Kriendler took me first to the famous wine cellar and from there all through the place, culminating with his living quarters on the top floor. A closet door happened to be open and I saw hanging on a rod about thirty or forty identical striped trousers and thirty or forty identical dark gray coats and on the floor in a row thirty or forty identical pairs of black shoes. I was impressed! Very rich men in Vienna owned perhaps six or eight identical suits, but thirty! That could happen only in America.

Miller, who liked his friends to appear as exalted as possible, introduced me as "Doctor Preminger." In Europe someone who holds a degree in law as I do is called doctor. I was aware that Americans restrict that title to those with medical degrees and protested to Miller. "You don't understand," he told me, "Americans are impressed by titles more than anybody else in the world." To this day many of the staff at "21" call me Doctor: a small memorial to Gilbert Miller.

After lunch I went to the St. Regis Hotel, where a room had been reserved for me. In the elevator I encountered the Austrian poet Franz Werfel who had been in New York for several months. I asked him eagerly how he liked it. He shrugged. "How can you like a place where instead of pulling a chain you press a button?"

He only expressed, as I was soon to discover, the attitude of a great many European refugees who came to America eager to find fault with almost everything. Like a German actor who told me he couldn't stand it here because Americans did not know how to eat properly. "They cut their meat first and then put the knife down and switch the fork to the right hand," he said with disgust. "Barbarians!" I guess this kind of criticism was an expression of subconscious self-defense by the newcomers in order not to have to blame themselves if they did not make it here. I, on the other hand, fell from day to day deeper and deeper in love with my new country, and that includes my days of failure as well as my days of success.

# 2

## GIVE MY REGARDS TO GILBERT MILLER

I began rehearsing *Libel!* on the morning after my arrival in New York in the Henry Miller Theatre which Gilbert inherited from his father after whom it was named. We had an excellent cast of English actors. The leads were taken by Colin Clive and Joan Marion. Clive had made a name for himself in *Journey's End*, a successful play about World War I. An equally important part was played by Wilfrid Lawson who, besides being an excellent actor, had a peculiar talent. He could blush at will and did so several times during every performance, to the delight and applause of the audience.

My idea to improve my English by comparing the English and German versions of *Libel!* turned out to be fortuitous. If I could not understand what an actor said during rehearsals I knew he was addressing me because the lines were not in the play. My only remaining problem was to figure out what he wanted.

The Millers made me part of their busy social life. I went to parties almost every night. Gilbert introduced me all over New York as "the famous European director." Although almost no one had ever heard of this "famous director," I was received with respect and warmth.

It marked a high point in my prestige when Jules Bache,

Miller's father-in-law, made me a regular at the Sunday luncheons in his magnificent town house at 814 Fifth Avenue.

There, one Sunday, I expressed my admiration for Franklin D. Roosevelt. I was never invited again.

After dinner I made the rounds of night clubs with Féfé Ferry and his friend Louis Shurr. Féfé was charming and funny, the most endearing of companions, but I soon discovered a sad weakness in his nature. He had such need to be accepted by famous and successful people that he went to any lengths to please them with an almost tragic disregard for his own dignity. Because he made such a humble servant of himself, he was often exploited by the very people he worshiped.

He telephoned me one night around two in a terrible state. He said he had to talk to me at once. He arrived shortly after I sleepily agreed and told me that a terrible thing had just happened to him.

"Imagine!" he cried, "I was at the _____ party"—naming a very social and rich man—"and after dinner I went to the guest bathroom. Just as I was shutting the door, someone grabbed the knob on the other side."

A look of horror appeared on his face. "It was the hostess! And I could not stop her. She seduced me right then and there."

"Congratulations!" I roared, laughing. But Féfé saw no humor in the situation. "How can you not see how serious this is?" he moaned. "If her husband finds out I will never be invited again to their house."

There was nothing I could say to console him. He could not imagine a more terrible fate than to be dropped from a guest list.

Louis, generally known as Doc Shurr, was an agent and an excellent one, totally devoted to his clients. When Zorina, who was one of them, had a fight with Paramount and was replaced by Ingrid Bergman in Hemingway's *For Whom the Bell Tolls*, he grieved so much that he couldn't eat or sleep for weeks and became seriously ill.

Shurr was an enchanting man right out of Damon Runyon. Small, homely, and bald, he loved to be seen with women who were tall, beautiful, and invariably very blond. He owned a white ermine cape which he took with him on dates. When he called for the girl he draped the cape around her shoulders, when he took her home he stood on his toes, kissed her good night, and gently retrieved the cape. Doc Shurr's real love was his secretary of many years who was never seen with him in public. She was neither blond nor tall nor beautiful but returned his love with true devotion. When he died he left her everything he had.

Whatever else occupied my nights I always ended up alone in one of the movie houses on Forty-second Street that played the same film over and over again. Homeless people spent their nights there sitting upright in front of the screen, sound asleep. I sat among them hour after hour, watching the same film at least three times. The first time the movie would be almost incomprehensible to me. I could catch only a few words here and there. During the second screening I could pick out sentences, and by the third time I understood most of the film. Another attempt to improve my English.

Gilbert Miller began rehearsing what was to become his biggest success, *Victoria Regina,* a few days after I had started rehearsals of *Libel!* One day he came to the threatre where I was working and took me aside. He opened by saying that without question he was matchless as director of intimate scenes. "There is no one in the world who can direct two or three actors as well as I can. But crowd scenes are different. I can't achieve my usual high standard when there are a lot of people on the stage," he confessed. "There's a scene toward the end of *Victoria Regina* where the stage is very crowded," he went on. "I'm having trouble with it. You're accustomed to handling big scenes like that." He was looking very unhappy. "Would you stage it for me?"

I was delighted to oblige. Gilbert pretended to be sick and stayed home for the next six days while I rehearsed the scenes in question. I had the opportunity to meet and direct Helen Hayes and Vincent Price. He acted later in several of my pictures and we became friends.

During my absence from *Libel!* rehearsals my stage manager,

Norris Houghton, took over. He later became one of the founders of the Phoenix Repertory Theatre in New York.

Gilbert Miller had agreed to let me use the same set in New York that was a big success in my Viennese production of *Libel!* It was the work of Otto Niedermoser, a young artist whom I discovered when he worked as assistant to Rudolf Strnad, one of the great European stage designers of all time.

I brought the plans and a model of Niedermoser's set with me to New York and an exact replica was constructed for the Broadway production. To my disgust the art directors union, however, insisted that one of its members be hired as the "set designer" and given credit for Niedermoser's work.

Niedermoser was a brave and high-principled man. When the Nazis invaded Austria he went immediately to the aid of his mentor Strnad's widow, who was Jewish. He hid her in his country house for six years, saving her life at the continuous risk of his own.

*Libel!* opened in Philadelphia at the Chestnut Street Opera House, a theatre which no longer exists. After two weeks we brought it to New York on the twentieth of December, 1935. It was a hit.

That night the jubilant cast gathered at Gilbert Miller's home to celebrate. It seemed an opportune time for me to bring up the matter of money. During the three months since I started to work for him Miller had never broached the subject to me and I was so pleased to have the chance to direct a play on Broadway that I hadn't mentioned it either.

"How much do you want?" he asked when I introduced the subject. "I'll leave it up to you," I said grandly.

Miller pondered a moment. "Would it be all right if I paid you the same salary that I paid Guthrie McClintic?" he asked.

I was flattered and astounded by Miller's offer. McClintic, one of the great American stage directors, had just brought *Winterset* to Broadway, a production which won the first plaque awarded by the New York Drama Critics Circle. He was undoubtedly the highest paid stage director in America.

I shook Miller's hand and thanked him warmly. Only later did I learn that McClintic had never worked as a director for Miller.

He was employed by him only during the earliest period of his career as stage manager.

*Libel!* ran for 159 performances in New York and would have lasted longer if not for the sudden death of its star, Colin Clive. By that time I was in Hollywood learning to direct films.

# 3

## A SMALL, FATAL ARGUMENT
## WITH DARRYL ZANUCK

I left New York a few days after the *Libell* opening, bound for
California on the fabulous transcontinental train, the *Super
Chief*. I was stunned by the sheer size of America and the
beauty of desert and mountains.

My first impression of Los Angeles was disappointing. I missed
the tall buildings of New York and the cosmopolitan feeling.
But Joseph Schenck had arranged a first-class welcome. A
chauffeured limousine took me from the train station to the
Beverly Wilshire Hotel where a suite filled with flowers and
champagne was waiting for me.

That night Schenck gave a glamorous party in my honor. I met
there Charlie Chaplin, Joan Crawford, Clark Gable, Louis B.
Mayer, Norma Shearer and her brilliant husband Irving Thal-
berg.

Schenck's big home was meant by some interior designer to be
impressive but it was rather tasteless. He had no interesting
paintings and the rooms were furnished in a mixture of chintz
and antiques placed against gloomy paneled walls.

When I was thanking my host and taking my leave, Schenck
put his hand on my shoulder. "Otto," he said, "this house will always be open to you. Any time you want to come to dinner,

don't even bother to phone. Just arrive. There will always be a plate for you on my table. As though you were my own son."

The following morning I was delivered by limousine to the Twentieth Century-Fox lot. It overwhelmed me. The only movie studio I had ever seen was a small one-stage affair in a suburb of Vienna. This one had at least a dozen stages, miles of Western streets, Georgian mansions and English Inns, teeming with a hubbub of Confederate soldiers, circus performers, Indians in war paint, cavaliers, and women in satin evening gowns, all of it guarded by an attendant at the gate who waved my studio car through with a royal gesture.

I had an appointment with Darryl F. Zanuck, the head of production. The big new administration building was still under construction. His temporary office was in a bungalow. I found him there, a short, restless, quick-eyed man too impatient to sit still. He had a polo mallet in his hand and while we talked he kept walking around the room, swinging at an imaginary ball.

Zanuck had started in films as a writer of Rin-Tin-Tin movies and worked himself up to become head of production at Warner Brothers. He left that studio to start Twentieth Century with Joseph Schenck which later became Twentieth Century-Fox. Despite the hectic pace of production, with film at every stage of completion all over the lot, he knew everything that was going on.

He opened the conversation by saying that Schenck had seen a few of my stage productions in Vienna and admired them very much. Schenck had seen none but I did not correct him. "However," Zanuck continued, "you haven't had much experience directing films. I suggest that for a while you watch another director at work. When you think you're ready, just let me know." He summoned a young director, Sidney Lanfield, who was working on *Sing, Baby, Sing*. I was to watch him and familiarize myself with American movie techniques.

Lanfield hated the arrangement from the start. Apparently he suspected that Zanuck was planning to replace him with me. It added to his aggravation that in my eagerness to learn I was at his elbow from his arrival on the set in the morning to his nighttime viewing of the dailies. Eventually he couldn't stand the sight of me. Everything I did irritated him. One day I was standing with my hands in my pockets just as he was about to start a scene. He turned to me in a fury. "You're making a noise!" he shouted. "You're playing with the coins in your pockets!" My pockets were empty.

Several weeks later Zanuck called me into his office and asked if I was ready to direct my first film. I said yes.

At that time each studio produced two types of films. The big-budget films had first-rate actors and the best directors. They were turned out carefully and relatively slow, since prestige and much of the profits depended on them. The low-budget films were churned out like sausages. Destined for the second half of double bills, they were routine productions that reflected the lesser talents that went into them. Studios used them also as testing ground for new actors and directors.

Zanuck had total authority over everything on the lot but personally supervised only the big-budget films. The others, called B pictures, were under a second executive producer, Sol Wurtzel, who was nicknamed the King of the B's.

I expected to start with a B picture so I was not disappointed when Zanuck told me to report to Wurtzel. My first film would be a production starring the famous baritone Lawrence Tibbett.

I was flattered and was about to thank Zanuck for trusting me with such an important artist, but he cut me short. "I signed that Tibbett for a lot of money to do two pictures," he snapped, striding back and forth between a piano and his big mahogany desk with his polo mallet swinging. "His first picture, *Metropolitan,* was a total flop. Total! I tried to settle his contract but he insists on being paid fully." He took a vicious swipe with the mallet. "We're stuck with the son of a bitch. There's no chance he'll ever be a success in films so you go ahead and practice on him."

It wasn't the most encouraging beginning but I went to work. The film was entitled *Under Your Spell* and had two writers assigned to it, Frances Hyland and Saul Elkins. John Stone acted as Wurtzel's associate producer.

We four, Stone, the writers, and I, worked on the script, reporting our progress from time to time to Wurtzel. He would listen to us in his office with his shoes off, his feet on the desk and a radio turned low to a football or baseball game. Whenever something on the radio caught his attention he leaned forward and turned the volume up full blast. We waited in silence until the action was over and we had his partial attention again. I thought it a bizarre way to conduct a script conference but Stone and the others seemed to find it quite natural.

When we were ready to begin shooting Tibbett took me aside. "I'm only doing this picture for the money," he informed me. "I'm sorry for you, since it isn't your fault, but I intend to work strictly according to my contract. It provides that I stop work at five o'clock. So be prepared. At five o'clock I quit."

In spite of the war between Zanuck and Tibbett, the work progressed quite well. As soon as Tibbett's scenes were done he'd sit down at the piano and sing for us. The actors, stagehands, and I liked him very much. The film didn't turn out too badly. The score was written by Howard Dietz and Arthur Schwartz. The title song, *Under Your Spell*, became a hit, which helped at the box office. When Zanuck saw the picture he was delighted. He praised me warmly and promoted me on the spot to the A-picture unit.

My first assignment in the big league was called *Nancy Steele Is Missing*. For the starring role Zanuck had borrowed Wallace Beery from Metro-Goldwyn-Mayer. Beery had won an Academy Award a few years earlier for *The Champ*, the picture which made young Jackie Cooper a star, and his *Tugboat Annie* with Marie Dressler had been a fabulous success.

I was looking forward to meeting Beery but, without any explanation, he failed to appear at our first appointment. Gregory Ratoff, an actor whose peculiar function was to be Zanuck's emissary to stars and directors, came to see me. "Beery won't do the picture with you," he informed me sadly. Ratoff could look more mournful than anybody I have ever known. "He says he won't make a film with a director whose name he can't pronounce."

And that was the end of *Nancy Steele Is Missing* as far as I was concerned.

Zanuck had another assignment for me, a comedy starring Edward Everett Horton and Zanuck's latest French import, Simone Simon. She had just come from France and her English was heavy with accent, which made her entirely wrong for that picture. It was called *Danger, Love at Work* and was one of those

Ingo and Otto Preminger

Otto, Ingo, mother and father on vacation in the Austrian Mountains

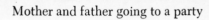
Mother and father going to a party

Mother and father taking a walk

Otto Preminger, age eighteen, Vienna

Otto and Ingo

Otto in a play in Vienna, 1925

fast-talking comedies popular at the time. The lines had to be delivered with snap or else they wouldn't work.

I protested to Zanuck that Simone was miscast but he wouldn't listen. "She'll do it," he told me. "You'll see, she'll be fine."

Obediently I went to work. Three days later Zanuck called me and Simone into his office. "I've just seen the rushes. You have no talent whatever. Go back to Paris," he said to her brutally. She got up and said with perfect calm and dignity, "Thank you, Mr. Zanuck," and left.

A few months later Zanuck brought her back. She became a big star, making a string of very successful pictures for him.

Zanuck replaced her in *Danger, Love at Work* with Ann Sothern, a good, professional actress. We finished the picture on schedule and again Zanuck was full of praise for my work.

My status was changing from an untried employee to a favorite. He had signed me to a standard seven-year contract with yearly options. It was time for the first renewal and he gave me a hefty raise. In addition I no longer lunched in the commissary but with him and other favorites in the executive dining room.

He also started inviting me to his house for dinner. There was a remarkable grapevine at the studios which conveyed instantly to everyone which people the studio heads were singling out for what was the highest honor possible: an invitation to their homes. It was like being knighted. Word of the invitation preceded the fortunate guest to the studio the following morning. The gate attendants leaped to admit him. There was awe in the manner of secretaries and a kind of deference in everyone encountered.

The reaction was understandable, considering the power that studio heads possessed. The careers of everyone depended on the whim of the man at the head, such as Zanuck at Fox, Harry Cohn at Columbia, Louis B. Mayer at MGM. On an impulse they could make an employee rich and famous or throw him out. They owned the film industry. Not just the studios but also the movie theatres. There was no competition. If an outsider took the gamble and made a picture, they would refuse to show it in their theatres.

Only two independent producers existed at that time and both had special status. One was Sam Goldwyn, who dropped out of

MGM after being one of its founders. The terms of his resignation included the guarantee that MGM theatres would exhibit his films. The other independent was David O. Selznick, who was Louis B. Mayer's son-in-law. This relationship assured him access to theatres.

It was therefore a matter of survival for people in Hollywood to keep themselves informed about who was in the good graces of the studio heads and who was not. My regular invitations to Zanuck's home put me in the category of the highly desirables. The rumor machine at Fox, which was very efficient, spread the word that I was marked for big things.

One day Gregory Ratoff came to me in great excitement, bubbling over with good news.

"You are going to direct the biggest film that this studio has ever made," he announced joyfully. "The biggest film this studio will ever make! The biggest budget in history: $750,000!" That was an extraordinary budget in those days.

Ratoff would say no more. Zanuck would break the news to me officially in a few days, he told me conspiratorially. Although I knew that he acted on Zanuck's instructions, he was so affectionate and guileless that I became very fond of him.

Like Féfé Ferry, Ratoff derived his sense of importance from the company he kept. He reveled in his role as Zanuck's confidant and messenger. The arrangement suited Zanuck very well because he could test reactions of his directors and stars through Ratoff without actually committing himself.

Ratoff was a good actor who later became a good director. I felt his relationship with Zanuck was rather demeaning but I could to some extent understand it. Part of the reason was that Ratoff's confidence in himself was undermined by his wife, the Russian actress Eugenie Leontovich. They had come to America together as refugees but she was the one with the greater reputation. She had been acclaimed in London for her performance in the play *Tovarich* in which she costarred with Cedric Hardwicke.

For a while after their arrival all attention was on her, and Gregory had difficulty finding work. Then the situation changed. Zanuck met him, liked him, and signed him to a contract at Fox, while Eugenie was unemployed.

His friendship with Zanuck helped restore Ratoff's self-confidence. Gregory was glad to share Zanuck's strange working hours. Zanuck usually arrived at the studio around eleven-thirty in the morning and quite often stayed until three or four the next morning.

Gregory forced himself to constantly appear cheerful, concealing the real Ratoff from most of the people around him. He feared that he would be rejected if he didn't perpetually amuse others. He used to confess to me sometimes that he felt depressed and yet half an hour later I found him in the executive dining room telling jokes and stories to keep Zanuck laughing.

The day after Gregory had given me the news about my pending assignment, Zanuck called me to his office. He was almost as excited as Ratoff had been. The film was to be based on Robert Louis Stevenson's classic *Kidnapped*. Zanuck would produce it personally, something he did only when he expected the picture to be sensational, and I would be the director. After only two films I was getting the plum assignment at Fox.

I had never heard of *Kidnapped*. Zanuck gave me a copy of the book and the script, which had been written under his supervision. He told me to read both and then report back to him.

Ratoff kept calling me every hour as I waded through them. "Isn't the script terrific!" he chortled. "Isn't it a marvelous story! Aren't you crazy about it?"

I was not. As I read it my heart sank. The story is set in the Scottish highlands, a part of the world totally strange to me, who was raised in Vienna, Austria. The place and the people were so far from my experience that I had no understanding at all of them. I began to realize that it would be a terrible mistake for me to attempt the picture. I told Ratoff that I couldn't do it.

He was shocked. "You can't refuse Zanuck!" he exclaimed. "You can't turn down this great chance. He'll never forgive you. You'll be signing your own death warrant."

His distress was real and touching. "Greesha," I told him gently, "I can't. It's wrong for me and I'm wrong for it."

"You *must* do it," he insisted. "Either do it or else pack your bags for Vienna. Because you will be finished here."

After a day and a night of arguing, he finally persuaded me that I better keep my doubts to myself. I agreed to do the picture. I met my cast. The key role of the boy was played by Freddie Bartholomew, who, at thirteen, had become a star as a result of his sensitive performance as David Copperfield.

Warner Baxter was also in the cast. He was one of the few silent picture stars who had been able to make the transition into talkies.

When I began shooting, Zanuck was in New York. He returned after a few days and asked at once to see the dailies. I was summoned to his office. He knew, as I knew, that the picture wasn't going well. He kept harping on a particular scene, one in which the boy says goodbye to his dog.

"I don't like the cuts you've made in that scene," he told me coldly. "That's a very touching moment in the script. I am the producer. You have no right to make cuts."

"Darryl," I said, surprised, "I didn't make any cuts in that scene." That was all Zanuck needed to release his anger and frustration. He exploded. We were in his new office in the administration building at Fox, which had just been completed. It was an enormous room, perfect for his pacing with the polo mallet. He stopped in front of me, pulled himself up to all the height he could muster, and started to shout.

"Do you mean to tell me that I don't know my own script?"

He whirled and ran to a revolving shelf containing copies of all the scripts currently in production. He spun it around furiously, looking for the *Kidnapped* script. He was so worked up that he couldn't locate it at first, which added to his rage. When he found it at last he pulled it out and shook it at me.

Now we were both shouting. "Look at it!" I yelled. "You'll see that I have not cut a word!"

He began to suspect he was mistaken, which made him even wilder. He ordered me out of his office. His secretaries were cowering in the anteroom. They had never before heard anyone shout back at Zanuck.

The next day Gregory Ratoff came to see me at my home. "It is very serious," he told me in funereal tones. "You can save yourself only if you immediately write a letter of apology to Zanuck."

"Certainly not," I said. "I have nothing to apologize for. If I'm through at Fox I'll work somewhere else."

Ratoff regarded me with sorrow. He shook his head. "If you

don't patch this up with Zanuck you'll never again work anywhere in Hollywood."

I didn't believe him but it turned out to be true. Studio heads
always closed ranks against anyone who had offended one of
them, unless the offender was a famous star or director. In that
case they would forget their solidarity. Unhappily I was not considered important enough to affront Zanuck by hiring me.

I slowly realized the dimension of my catastrophe. It was
significant that even my friend Ratoff saw me from now on only
at my home where Zanuck's lackeys could not discover our meetings and report them to their boss.

At the studio there were no more invitations to the executive
dining room. I ate in the commissary alone, avoided like the
plague by almost everybody. My parking space was moved to
the farthest corner of the back lot. I went to my office every day
but the telephone never rang. One day I arrived to find my name
had been removed from the door and the lock changed.

After that I stayed home. Zanuck's executive assistant, Lou
Schreiber, called me and informed me coldly that I was breaking
my contract by not coming to the studio.

"You've taken away my office," I protested. "What do you
want me to do, sit on your doorstep?"

My contract posed an interesting problem for Zanuck. He had
just taken up my first option with a big increase in salary. It was
going to be expensive for Fox to keep me idle for eleven months.

I took no satisfaction from the situation. I wanted to work. I
decided to contact Joseph Schenck and offer him my resignation.
After all he was the one who had brought me from Vienna.

I telephoned Schenck's office for an appointment. His secretary said he was busy that day. I telephoned the next day and
the next. Every day she had another explanation why the man
who asked me to consider myself his son could not see me. Finally his secretary and I developed a friendly, amused relationship. I kept on telephoning her daily and she chuckled at the
excuses she was inventing.

I asked Louis Shurr, who had an office in Hollywood, to repre-
sent me as my agent. He went to every studio trying to find work
for me, but as Ratoff had predicted, the doors were shut. Shurr
was a friend of Buddy De Sylva's, a former song-writer who was

head of Paramount. He went to see him and I instructed Shurr to say that I would take anything. "Tell him I'll even direct tests."

De Sylva, whom I had met socially, didn't dare incur Zanuck's anger but he was very tactful. His message was that I was too talented to be wasted as a test director. As soon as something worthy of my ability came along, he'd call me. He never did.

There was only one thing left for me: the stage. I concentrated on finding a property that I could direct on Broadway. I spent my days reading manuscripts and books.

Meanwhile, *Kidnapped* was completed by another director, Alfred Werker. It was one of the biggest flops that Twentieth Century-Fox ever had, and they had quite a few.

When my eleven months' well-paid bondage to Fox was over I packed my things and headed East, back to Broadway where I had started my life in America so hopefully just two years earlier. Friends suggested, and meant it kindly, I should keep going. My old job at the beautiful Josefstadt theatre in Vienna could be mine for the asking. I would once again be surrounded by friends and admirers.

Though I had never in my life known as dark a time as that winter of 1937, I didn't for a second consider leaving America. I loved the country. I believed in my future. I had no desire at all to return to Vienna, not ever. Events proved I was right.

# 4

## STAGE-STRUCK IN VIENNA

My father, Mark Preminger, was born on January 15, 1877, in Czernowitz, the capital of Bukowina, the most eastern province of the Austrian-Hungarian Empire. His parents were very poor devout Jews. His father, an intelligent man, a Talmudic scholar, wanted him to have a first-rate education.

He was brilliant and had no difficulty leading his class every year, even though he had to work around the clock to support himself and—after his father's untimely death—his mother and five sisters. He graduated cum laude as doctor of law. Because his marks were the highest in the country he was awarded the ring that was presented yearly to the Empire's best student: a very large sapphire surrounded by twenty-eight diamonds. The Emperor Franz Josef's initials are set in small diamonds on the sapphire. The ring is now with my brother's son, Jim.

Austria is a Roman Catholic country and was always anti-Semitic, long before Hitler. Only extremely able Jews could succeed in law or medicine by being the best in their field and discreet about their Jewishness, which people in need of their superior skills were willing to overlook. A famous mayor of Vienna, Dr. Lueger, coined a phrase which describes it perfectly. He said: "I determine who is Jewish and who is not."

My father joined the Emperor's legal department. His rise was rapid. A few years later, when the position of Chief Prosecutor (about the equivalent of Attorney General in the United States) became vacant, he was, in spite of his youth, an obvious candidate. But no Jew had ever held this post in the history of the Empire. He was summoned to the Minister of Justice who informed him that he was chosen for this important job; he had only to convert to Catholicism. This was not an unusual request. Many Jews converted for lesser reasons of expediency. Nevertheless, my father refused. Even though he had not practiced his religion since his student days, the demand to change it offended a deep-rooted principle in his nature. To his surprise he was given the post anyway. Since this made him the Empire's chief legal defender he was in a position of great power, which included censorship of the press. At the age of twenty-six he married my mother, Josepha Fraenkel, who was seven years younger than he. She was sweet, warm-hearted, and easily worried. Her father owned a lumberyard and her grandfather, a serene, unpretentious man, had a large horse and cattle farm where I spent several summers of my childhood. I was their firstborn and my parents named me Otto Ludwig. One set of documents lists Vienna as my birthplace but another set, equally valid-looking, places my birth at my great-grandfather's farm some distance away. One records that I was born on the fifth of December, 1906, the other exactly one year earlier. At my time of life one year more or less makes little difference.

My father believed that it was impossible to be too kind or too loving to a child. He never punished me. When there were problems he sat down and discussed them with me reasonably, as though I was an adult. I don't think my mother agreed completely with this method but she acted, as always, according to his wishes. I adored him. Even now, more than twenty years after his death, I often think of him in the present tense. Sometimes I have the impulse to call him and talk to him as though he was still alive. I often remember and follow in my daily activities some of the advice he gave me. For instance, he cautioned me against seeking vengeance. He thought it was a waste of time. "Don't pursue your enemies," he used to say. "It would only aggravate you. Let them be. God will take care of them eventually."

I was five years old when my brother Ingo was born. We always were and still are very close.

My interest in sex started at the age of seven. A girl cousin of mine, also seven, took me one day to the stables on our great-grandfather's farm. There we watched with curiosity how horses copulated. We secretly tried to imitate what we had observed but we failed, despite our diligent efforts.

In 1914, World War I began with the assassination of Archduke Franz Ferdinand, heir to the throne of the Empire. My father was made chief military prosecutor. His new duties took him to Graz, capital of the province of Styria. There some ten thousand people were confined in a concentration camp under suspicion of plotting against the Empire. It was his task to sort out those prisoners who should stand trial and free those wrongfully arrested. Since these decisions would occupy the better part of a year, he took his family with him.

I was eight years old. My parents enrolled me in a public school. There I had a frightful experience.

Graz was even more anti-Semitic than Vienna. In my school the day began with Roman Catholic prayers and religious instruction. I sat silent during the reciting. One day at recess a classmate asked me what my religion was. "Jewish," I answered. That afternoon on my way home a group of older boys who had been waiting in a recessed doorway grabbed me, pulled me in, and beat me savagely. They cursed me and called me names I had never heard before. After what seemed an eternity they ran away, leaving me on the floor. I limped home with my face bleeding, my clothes torn. The emotion I felt was shame. It seemed to me that I had disgraced my father, that the beating was a reflection on him. I didn't want anybody to know about it. I told my parents that I had slipped and fallen. I learned only years later that they had realized at once what had happened. Without mentioning it to me my father went to the school principal to complain. He must have been impressed by my father's high rank. Though he said there was nothing he could do, I was not attacked again.

Soon after we returned to Vienna our family doctor discovered during a routine checkup that I had a heart murmur. He recommended that I avoid strenuous exercises and sports. My mother was exceedingly alarmed, although she was told that it was not a serious matter. Actually, the heart murmur has never bothered me. At the beginning of World War II, when I filled in my questionnaire for the draft board in Los Angeles, I neglected to list it. I had forgotten its existence. The medical examiner, however, noticed the defect and classified me 4-F.

My father was in the most dramatic period of his career during the First World War. Big trials of important politicians and functionaries accused of treason and conspiracy against the Empire were taking place in Vienna.

Eduard Beneš, who became the first President of Czechoslovakia when that country was created after the war, was one of the defendants my father prosecuted. With him were a number of others who later formed Beneš' first cabinet. Depending on the point of view, they were Czech patriots or Austrian traitors. My father, according to his official position, held the latter opinion. His analysis of their conspiracy was so perceptive and accurate that his summations are still being used by scholars of history.

After the war was lost and the Empire fell apart my father was attacked and abused by the newspapers of the new Austrian Republic because he had been prominent during the Habsburg regime.

One day he found my mother weeping over a cruel editorial. He comforted her with words that left a deep impression on me. "Will you never learn, darling?" he said. "Anyone who acts in public must be prepared for criticism, just or unjust. Only your own conviction and your own judgment of yourself count."

I was twelve and did not realize that I would spend my adult life surrounded by critics. When I am under attack I shrug off what people say against me. That is, if I believe they are wrong.

My father opened a private practice in criminal law and soon was one of the most successful lawyers in the country.

The heart murmur did one thing for me. Isolated from other boys and their outdoor games, I became a passionate reader. Particularly the classics appealed to me. I also discovered that I had a quick memory. This skill demanded an audience. I made myself a pest reciting Shakespeare, Goethe, and Schiller with untiring enthusiasm. My maternal grandfather, the kindest of men, patiently listened for hours and praised me. I became so obsessed with theatre that I almost ceased attending school. I spent most of my days in Vienna's beautiful National Library reading plays. When I wasn't there I undoubtedly was attending a film or a play or an opera. On my thirteenth birthday my understanding grandfather gave me a season ticket to the State Theatre.

In order to explain my absences from school I had to write notes forging my father's signature. In fact I still sign my name the way he did. Eventually I was discovered when a teacher called my mother to inquire about my health after a continuous absence of more than ten weeks. My mother was shocked but my father reacted calmly. "I used to skip school too, my dear," he told her. He sat down with me and talked without recrimination or moralizing. He called the school and told them that I was ill and would probably recover in about a week. Then he hired a tutor to help me catch up with my studies.

I suppose I was sexually precocious. At thirteen I fell for a famous actress, Leopoldine Konstantin, who, with her German industrialist boyfriend, was a frequent guest in our house. She was the first professional to hear me recite. She was very encouraging and predicted a great career for me. I adored her. One evening she had to leave early after dinner because she was in rehearsals. My father asked me to take her home in our car. I sat next to her, fighting the whole way against my desire to fondle her knee. I was tortured by frustration but I didn't have the guts to do it.

When I was fourteen I fell in love with a girl of the same age. Eva and I met in dancing class. While neither of us had any experience with sex we knew enough to recognize what our longings were about. We decided to have an affair. First I had to find a place. I rented a cheap, shabbily furnished room in a suburb. We met there in the afternoons. But neither Eva nor I knew how to proceed. Therefore I bought a textbook on anatomy which was as close as bookstores came to a sex manual at that time. Though we studied the book intensely it took several meetings over a two-week period until we succeeded. It is not easy for two virgins to determine where all the limbs go.

Unfortunately, Eva kept a diary. Her mother found it, read it, and went at once to see my father. I was working at my desk and my mother was nearby sewing when he came in and told her that I had seduced Eva. My mother was aghast. "What did you tell the girl's mother?" My father could hardly suppress a proud smile. "I advised her to watch her daughter," he said. "She could not expect me to watch my son."

Eva's parents took his suggestion literally. After that she was never without an escort. For a while I trailed behind her broken-hearted when she went to school, but I was not allowed to approach her.

Many years later when I was appearing on Broadway in *Margin for Error*, she sent a note backstage. We met and she introduced me to her husband with whom she had opened a travel agency when they moved to New York in 1938.

It was an awkward reunion. She seemed to be still nursing her memory of our romance but, sadly, I felt nothing. If her parents had allowed our affair to run its natural course she would have been free of me. Because we were separated so abruptly, she was haunted by the sense of something she missed, something unfinished.

A few years later her husband telephoned to tell me that she had died of a heart attack in the Mideast while conducting a tour for their travel agency.

# 5

## MAX REINHARDT, MARLENE DIETRICH, AND HEDY

I made my first appearance on a stage at the age of twelve reciting poems at a charity concert that otherwise featured only adults. The applause I received reinforced my secret decision to become an actor. My parents were proud of my success but did not take my passion for the theatre seriously. They assumed it was a child's dream and would pass. In 1923, when I was not quite seventeen, Vienna went wild with excitement at the news that Max Reinhardt would open a theatre in Vienna. Austrian by birth, he had left for Berlin as a young man and was now at the age of fifty internationally acknowledged as the world's greatest stage director.

At this point, Camillo Castiglioni, a multimillionaire who loved the theatre, made Reinhardt the following offer: he would provide unlimited funds for the purchase and renovation of a theatre in Vienna. In return he asked only that the best and biggest box be reserved for him at every performance. Castiglioni was born the son of a rabbi in Milan. He came to Vienna in 1918 at the end of the First World War. In a short time he made a huge fortune by shrewd manipulations in the international money market. Reinhardt accepted his offer without hesitation. Unlimited funding was exactly the budget that suited him best. He purchased the Theater in der Josefstadt which, once beautiful, was now 135 years old and in bad repair. He engaged a well-known architect, Karl Witzman, and ordered him to preserve the perfect acoustics and the beautiful baroque style of the old building. Everything else was transformed according to Reinhardt's brilliant imagination with the help of Castiglioni's open purse. The building next door was purchased and remodeled into a restaurant with luxurious foyers where theatre patrons could stroll, eat, and drink during intermissions and after the performance. The most beautiful detail Reinhardt added was a large crystal chandelier made in Venice. It hangs brightly lit in the middle of the theatre as the audience arrives. When the performance is about to start its eight hundred electric candles dim slowly while the huge glittering fixture rises to the ceiling in order to give the boxes and balconies an unobstructed view of the stage. This beautiful effect creates in the audience a unique mood of expectation.

All Vienna was following the restoration of the old theatre with delight but no one was more excited than I. I wrote a letter to Reinhardt asking for an audition. I gave General Delivery as my return address because I was afraid my parents would not approve of my trying to get into the theatre while I was still in school.

For six weeks I went three times a day to the post office to ask if there was a letter for me. Then I gave up. About a month later I went back—just in case. I found an answer to my letter. It came from Dr. Stefan Hock, one of Reinhardt's top associates, granting me an appointment. The date for it, however, had passed by two days. Now I started to hang around the stage door trying to see Dr. Hock. I had to be alert not to be spotted by my teachers, who frequently walked by the theatre, for my school was located only about fifty yards from the stage door. They were supposed to believe that I was ill and confined to my bed. Eventually Dr. Hock received me in the makeshift office he was using while the rebuilding was going on. I auditioned for him to the sound of wild hammering. He listened, said nothing, got up and took me to a large room where Reinhardt sat surrounded by about a dozen people. "Now read for the Professor," Hock said. That is what everybody called Reinhardt. I was very nervous but gave a good reading. For Reinhardt nodded his approval to Hock,

who took me back to his office and congratulated me for having
become the first apprentice actor of the Viennese Reinhardt
Company. I did not quite know what "apprentice actor" meant
but I was overjoyed.

Now I had to break the news to my parents. My father was
torn between pride in my accomplishment and disapproval of
my decision to become an actor. However, he behaved graciously as usual, congratulated me, and said I was intelligent
enough to decide for myself what I wanted to do with my life.
He made one request. "As a personal favor to me," he said,
"please finish some formal studies. I don't care what field you
choose, but obtaining a degree will be useful to you later in life
no matter what you do." He still hoped I would eventually
change my mind. I chose law. At the University of Vienna students did not have to attend classes and lectures. They could
study at home as long as they presented themselves at appointed
times over a period of four years for a total of six exams required
for a doctor of law degree. My father provided me with tutors
and I arranged my education to suit my theatrical schedule.

Reinhardt had chosen Carlo Goldoni's *The Servant of Two
Masters* for the opening performance of his new theatre. He
mounted it in the commedia dell'arte style. Scenery changes were
accomplished in front of the audience by actors in costume mov-
ing in dance step to music by Mozart while they carried chairs,
tables, sofas, and other props on and off the stage. As one of the
young furniture movers I made my acting debut.

On opening night, April 1, 1924, the audience was almost as
dazzling as the all-star cast. Austria's finest turned out to see
what had been accomplished by Reinhardt's genius and Castiglioni's millions.

Soon I discovered that the Professor's concept of the apprentice actor did not include much acting. He had only insignificant
small parts for me during that first season of four plays. However, he made me his assistant at the acting school he opened in
the exquisite intimate theatre the Austrian government had put
at his disposal in the former imperial summer palace at
Schönbrunn, a suburb of Vienna. He did not employ the usual
breed of acting teachers, who are mostly disillusioned actors or
directors who did not succeed in their chosen profession or peo-

ple who studied history and theory of the stage but never acted
or directed and therefore are not capable of teaching the craft of
acting. Every teacher at the Reinhardt Seminar, as the school
was named, was an accomplished and active actor or director. In
many cases they were the most prominent members of the Reinhardt Ensemble. Years later, when I succeeded Reinhardt at the
Josefstadt I also took over his school.

After the first few months in Vienna Reinhardt also made me
his assistant—one of about two dozen—at the Salzburg Festival,
which he founded. It is still a yearly fixture and big attraction of
Austria's tourist season. Although it was considered a great
honor to be one of Reinhardt's assistants, I grew more and more
restless and frustrated because I wanted to act. At Salzburg,
Reinhardt staged a huge pantomime: *The Miracle*. There were
no professional extras available. Therefore the five hundred nuns
marching in a long procession were played by society women
and other amateurs. The Professor made me dress in a nun's costume so I could march with them and lead them. It was not the
kind of role I had been dreaming about.

Still, it was fascinating to watch him at work. If he felt that an
actor resisted his direction he would back off and let him do as
he pleased. But if an actor wanted help he would give of himself
more than anyone I have ever seen. He'd find as many as ten
different ways to do a scene and demonstrate each one of them
tirelessly until he found the best one for that particular actor. As
he went along he invented more bits of business, more gestures
that enriched the character beyond anything the playwright had
imagined.

Not infrequently he became so absorbed in his creative zeal on
behalf of a minor character that he would add lines or entire
scenes to enlarge and deepen the part.

He was oblivious to the human limitations of his cast. Usually
rehearsals were scheduled for ten in the morning. Reinhardt did
not reach the theatre before two in the afternoon. Assistants
started rehearsals without him. He would watch or attend to
business for an hour or two and then, around four o'clock, he
took over. He knew how to create enthusiasm and excitement
even in an already tired cast.

He was still fresh by midnight, full of concentration and vitality, while the actors staggered with exhaustion. I remember one time he was rehearsing *The Merchant of Venice* at two in the morning. The cast had been working continuously for sixteen hours but Reinhardt was unaware of their fatigue. He was doing a scene with William Dieterle, who played one of Portia's suitors. He made him repeat the scene over and over for hours. Dieterle was young and strong but eventually dropped in a dead faint. While he was carried off the stage Reinhardt turned to the stage manager and said, "Next scene!"

He wasn't a cruel or callous man. What seemed like indifference to the distress of others was really Reinhardt's complete absorption by his work.

After a year with the Professor, watching and learning, I decided my career would advance better if I joined a company where I would have the opportunity to play important parts.

German theatre was mostly regional. Each city subsidized at least one theatre where repertory companies presented plays, operas, and operettas. Actors and singers were hired by the theatre managers for the coming season at auditions held in Berlin or Vienna during the late spring.

I joined that circuit. My first job was in Prague, a bilingual city which had a large German population and two German theatres. Since this was Czechoslovakia, where the Preminger name was not highly esteemed by the now powerful new leaders, many of whom my father had prosecuted for treason during the First World War, I used a stage name: Otto Pretori.

The following season I worked in Zürich, where I met Kurt Katsch who, fifteen years later, took over my part in the road company of Clare Boothe's *Margin for Error*.

I was nineteen years old and already losing my hair. My father had been bald at an early age but that was no consolation for an aspiring leading man. In desperation I went to a doctor. He told me if I shaved my head my hair would grow back thicker and healthier.

I arranged a two-month vacation in Brittany, France, where nobody knew me and followed the doctor's advice. I waited. My hair grew in slowly at the sides and the back. It never returned to the top of my head.

Nevertheless I played the leading man in several productions at my next engagement: Aussig an der Elbe, a small German city in Czechoslovakia. The theatre was run by an actor-manager, Alfred Huttig. I asked him to give me a chance to direct. His kindness was especially remarkable because the young singer he loved left him soon after I joined the company and became my companion.

I returned to Vienna at the end of that season. I decided not to act any more, only to direct.

I founded a theatre with an actor, Rolf Jahn, as my partner. His wife was a wealthy stage-struck countess who used the stage name Marita Streelen. She put up the money and played the leads. We called the theatre Die Komödie. It still exists. Our opening production was Chekhov's masterpiece *The Three Sisters*. One of them, naturally, was the countess.

The afternoon of opening night I had to report to the University to take the last of my law exams. It was a disaster. I flunked the exam and the play I had directed was a miserable failure. Both on the same day.

Three months later I tried the exam again, passed it, and received my Doctor of Law degree. At about the same time I directed my first hit in Vienna, a play set in a courtroom. I'm attracted to courtroom dramas, possibly because I spent so much of my youth fascinated by the trials my father conducted.

While I was at Die Komödie, Marlene Dietrich appeared at another theatre in Vienna. She played a small part in the American play *Broadway*. I saw her and thought she was an exciting prospect for our company. My partner, however, and his wife, the countess, said Marlene had no talent and would never get anywhere. We had a rule that all decisions about the theatre had to be unanimous, so she wasn't signed. Instead she went to Berlin and appeared in a revue, wearing for the first time a man's white tie and tails. Josef von Sternberg saw her there and put her in *The Blue Angel*. She most probably would have become a great star anyway, but if my partner and his wife had liked her better it would have taken her a while longer.

After one season Rolf Jahn and I parted. My next enterprise was a very large popular theatre which formerly had been used for opera productions. This time my backer was the sister of an excellent actor, Jacob Feldhammer. She was married to a rich industrialist and was fascinated by the theatre.

I found a number of talented young actors, among them Oskar Homolka, who, at twenty-four, became an instant success in a play based on the American film *Underworld.*

The season was uneven but ended profitably with *The Sachertorte,* a big comedy hit. The author, Siegfried Geyer, was a prominent critic and good friend of mine, a rare, practically unique combination. Although my contract gave me artistic autonomy, Feldhammer's sister started to exert more and more influence by suggesting plays and her brother wanted to play all the good parts. It became a situation very much like a year earlier with Rolf Jahn and his countess. I resigned.

Meantime, Max Reinhardt's theatre was in serious financial trouble. It was a period of raging inflation. Austria's and Germany's currencies had collapsed. Camillo Castiglioni lost his fortune and could no longer pay for Reinhardt's artistically successful but financially unrealistic productions. His Berlin production of *Die Fledermaus,* for instance, played to capacity for several months and yet lost a great deal of money because the running costs were higher than the theatre's capacity. To add to the problems, Max Reinhardt's brother Edmund, who was the business head of the family and the administrator of his theatres, died. He had been the only one who could sometimes restrain his brother's excesses.

Castiglioni had watched me during my first two seasons in Vienna. He suggested to Reinhardt to engage me as director at the Josefstadt. Reinhardt agreed and I accepted with enthusiasm. My first production was again a courtroom drama: *Voruntersuchung* (Preliminary Inquiry) by Max Alsberg, a Berlin lawyer, and Otto Ernst Hesse. It was a hit. Next I did *The Front Page* by Ben Hecht and Charles MacArthur. The German title was *Reporter.* It was also a success and started the career of Paula Wessely, who became one of the most important German stage and film stars.

When the Nazis invaded Austria seven years later, Paula Wessely and her husband Attila Hoerbiger, also a member of the Josefstadt ensemble, took a frightful risk. They saved a friend, the Jewish actor and writer Hans Jaray, who had no passport.

They hid him in the trunk of their car and drove him across the border. Later they changed. They socialized with the top Nazis and gradually came not only to share the violent anti-Semitism of Hitler's cohorts but to exceed them in it. Both starred in Nazi propaganda films. Toward the end of the war, when it became obvious that Hitler was losing, she went mad with fear and tried to kill her two young daughters. Luckily they were saved. After several years in an institution she was released as cured and is now once more a top German star.

What do I feel about them and the many other friends of mine who behaved similarly? Hatred? No. Contempt? Perhaps. But mostly pity. Because they became, through the distortion of their sense of values and their loss of human dignity, victims of Hitler's madness just like the millions he actually murdered and tortured.

In 1932 Reinhardt withdrew from the management of his theatre in Berlin and notified Camillo Castiglioni that the 1932/33 season would be his last at the Josefstadt. In spite of fierce competition and my youth—I was only twenty-six—Castiglioni, who was the president of the corporation which owned the theatre, named me Reinhardt's successor. It caused quite a sensation in Vienna's theatrical circles.

Camillo Castiglioni was short, extremely fat, and not particularly attractive-looking. But he was bright, witty, and possessed a great deal of persuasive charm. He fell in love with a beautiful young actress, Iphigenia Buchman, and married her. She left the stage and lived with him in luxury as one of the leaders of Vienna's society. She attached herself particularly to the Reinhardts. When Castiglioni lost his fortune he also lost Iphigenia. When the Reinhardts left Vienna she left with them. Because there were no buyers for his large mansion during those early years of the Depression, Castiglioni continued to live in it though he had to sell his precious paintings, tapestries, and furniture. He kept, however, the huge entrance hall intact and one small room in which he worked, ate, slept, and received occasional visitors. I dined with him there frequently. He told me one evening that he most urgently needed a hundred thousand schillings, a sum that then was comparable to the same amount of dollars today. For about two weeks I worked very hard to obtain the money for him, but without success. At last Heinrich Haas, the same man who financed the first and only film I made in Vienna, loaned me the money for Castiglioni. I happily took it to him in one hundred crisp thousand-shilling notes. That evening we dined at his desk. When we finished, his only servant, now wearing a chauffeur's cap, reappeared and announced that the car was ready. His famous limousine with its extremely long custom-made body was another status symbol that Castiglioni had not parted with. "Where are we going?" I asked. "To Baden," Castiglioni announced. My heart sank. In Baden, a small resort town about forty minutes from Vienna, was one of the three casinos the government had licensed after the First World War in order to attract rich foreigners and help Austria's budgetary plight. When we arrived at the casino Castiglioni walked straight to the baccarat table. He started betting one thousand schillings each coup. He lost ninety-nine consecutive times. Then he threw the last thousand-schilling note on the table as tip for the croupier, turned to me and said without showing any emotion, "Let's go."

His life ended tragically. When Hitler invaded Austria, Castiglioni fled to his native Italy and managed to hide from Mussolini's henchmen in a monastery. He died there at the age of forty-eight.

Whether it was luck, instinct, or talent, at the end of my first season as head of the Josefstadt the theatre was showing a profit. At that time Reinhardt conceived the idea to direct four big all-star productions in quick succession at the Josefstadt and then take them on a tour through Europe. I was convinced that this would mean a step back into deficit and decided against it. His wife, Helene Thimig, a great actress and star and member of a famous theatrical family, came to see me. She was shocked. She and the Professor had thought I would be grateful to have these four Reinhardt productions in the theatre. I remained firm. "The theatre is my responsibility now," I told her. "I have planned my season. I won't change my plans." But I had a suggestion. If Reinhardt obtained financial backing independently I would move my productions to another theatre and he could rent the Josefstadt. The source of such independent backing was obvious. Reinhardt planned to cast as one of the leads in Schiller's *Maria*

*Stuart* a beautiful if not very talented actress named Eleonora von Mendelsohn. Her family's wealth was exceeded only by the Rothschilds. I recommended that she be asked to provide the money and she did. I moved my company into another theatre while Reinhardt prepared his four productions in the Josefstadt. The four plays and the following tour were a disaster and Eleonora von Mendelsohn lost a small fortune on the venture.

Eleonora was a very beautiful woman who always was in love with a famous man. Reinhardt was one of her infatuations and another was the conductor Arturo Toscanini. She went to extraordinary lengths in these curious, one-sided affairs. For instance when Toscanini visited her castle in Salzburg he paused to admire a priceless painting by Dürer. By the time he returned to his hotel room the picture was hanging there as a present from Eleonora. Another time, when she was living in New York, she got a friend, Count Ledebur, to drive her every morning to the house in the country where Toscanini was staying. Upon arrival the Count, who was six feet six inches tall, stood against the high white wall that surrounded the place. Eleonora climbed on his shoulders so she could catch a glimpse of the unsuspecting Toscanini taking his regular morning stroll in the garden.

Reinhardt was her guest on Long Island when he died on October 31, 1943. He was walking his dog, which was attacked by another one. Trying to separate them, Reinhardt exerted himself too much. He had a heart attack and died soon after.

Eleonora eventually married an actor. They lived in the Gladstone Hotel on Fifty-second Street with a male friend of his. One day she was found dead on a projecting roof many floors below their rooms. It was never established if she committed suicide or what caused her fall.

When Reinhardt left the Josefstadt in 1933 he promised to return every season to direct one play. After the failure of his costly tour he went to California to do *A Midsummer Night's Dream* in the Hollywood Bowl. He did many productions of that fantasy by Shakespeare, no two of them alike. One even had real trees and soil on the stage and Reinhardt perfumed the entire theatre to smell like a forest. It was a natural culmination that he would direct *A Midsummer Night's Dream* on film. While he was in California, Warner Brothers invited him to do so.

Because he had no experience in film-making, Warners offered Reinhardt a choice of two directors to assist him. One was Michael Curtiz, the other William Dieterle. Curtiz was an outstanding, established motion picture director. Dieterle had directed only a few unimportant films. But the Reinhardts knew him and liked him well. Influenced by his wife, Reinhardt chose Dieterle. Reinhardt's wife, Helene Thimig, lived in constant fear of losing Reinhardt. She screened everyone who approached him socially or professionally. She wanted around him only people who were her friends and made her feel safe. Though I was grateful to Reinhardt for giving me my start and admired him very much, I never became a member of the close circle. Helene did not approve of me because I was too outspoken. While Reinhardt was in California the theatre in Vienna continued to prosper. I established a pattern for plays that were successful. When they finished their run in the Josefstadt but still had life in them I moved them to one of Vienna's vacant theatres. At one time I had five productions on the boards simultaneously. We used one small theatre, the Kammerspiele, so frequently that it was eventually bought by the Josefstadt as a permanent satellite.

Before I took over the Josefstadt I had attempted a film, *Die Grosse Liebe* (The Great Love). It was financed by Heinrich Haas, the same merchant from Graz who loaned me the money for Castiglioni's night of baccarat. Though it had good reviews and earned a profit, I prefer to forget it.

One afternoon I was sitting in my office at the Josefstadt. My secretary, Miss Holmann, brought in a girl with a letter of introduction from a friend of mine, the Hungarian playwright Geza Herczeg, who later went to Hollywood and wrote several screenplays, among them, *The Life of Emile Zola.* I knew many beautiful women but I had never seen a lovelier face. The girl told me shyly that her name was Hedwig Kiesler, that she was called Hedy, that she was seventeen and wanted to act. I took her downstairs to the stage to meet Reinhardt, who was rehearsing a French play, *The Weaker Sex,* by Bourdet. He was as stunned by her as I was and gave her a small part immediately. Soon afterward she made the film *Ecstasy*, which became notorious because of a scene which showed her nude. When she married a multimillionaire munitions manufacturer, Fritz Mandl, he tried in vain to buy up and destroy every print of the film.

Hedy's next goal was Hollywood. She saw her opportunity when Reinhardt invited her and her husband to a party at his Salzburg castle in honor of Louis B. Mayer. Mayer was impressed by her beauty and invited her to come to London, where he would be staying for a few days. He suggested that they discuss a contract there.

She later described their meeting to me. It was exactly like my experience with Joseph Schenck. A hotel suite full of cigar smoke and men in shirt sleeves playing cards. He was no longer interested in her. He told Bob Ritchie, one of his assistants, to offer her the standard seven-year contract with six-month options, starting at a hundred and fifty dollars a week.

Hedy coldly refused. "I pay my chauffeur more," she told him and left.

She did not give up, however. She found out that Mayer was leaving by ship for the United States a few days later. She booked passage, first class, for herself and her little Viennese manager on the same voyage. She dressed up every day looking for Mayer all over. He never left his stateroom. On the day before the ship was to dock in New York he emerged at last. She placed herself casually in his path and pretended to be surprised to see him. He asked where she was going. "To the United States," she replied. "For which company?" he inquired, suddenly interested. "For no company," she said casually. Her evasive-sounding answer convinced Mayer that she was planning to sign with a rival, if she hadn't done so already. He invited her to have dinner with him. Hedy asked if she could bring her manager, whose presence on the ship made Mayer even more certain that she had an offer from one of his competitors.

That night Hedy dressed in the most glamorous gown she owned. She was almost ready when she was suddenly stricken by violent seasickness. When her manager arrived to escort her to Mayer's stateroom he found her prostrate on the bed, too miserable to move. He went to dinner without her, which was final proof to the MGM head that Hedy was committed to someone else. In order to test it he offered her manager a contract that

The Theater in der Josefstadt, Vienna (BRUNO REIFFENSTEIN)

In *Stalag 17*, 1953

Oskar Karlweis and Otto

Otto and his father

Otto, Hansi Niese, and Attila Hoerbiger in *Die Grosse Liebe*, 1931

Otto with his mother and father, October 16, 1935, at the station
leaving for America

Himself (LOTTE MEITNER-GRAF)

was unprecedented for a newcomer. The manager accepted. Mayer gave her a new name: Hedy Lamarr.

After my first season managing the Josefstadt the Austrian Minister of Art and Education offered me a contract to head the State Theatre in Vienna, the highest theatrical position in the country. The terms were agreed upon and the Minister invited me to his sumptuous office in the former Imperial Palace. He congratulated me and told me how happy he was to have a young man with my talent in this post. Then he asked me to give him the honor of being my witness at my conversion to Catholicism. "It is a mere formality," he said, "but no Jew ever held the office of Managing Director of Austria's State Theatre." I am not religious but without hesitation I refused, as my father did a generation before. The only difference was that he got the post, while in my case the Minister made polite conversation for a few more minutes. Then I left and never heard of the contract again.

My refusal to convert most likely saved my life. If I had accepted I would not have been a free agent two years later when Joseph Schenck invited me to Hollywood. I would have been in Vienna when Hitler invaded Austria in 1938 and would have met the same fate as many of my friends. Because, for Hitler, converted or not a Jew remained a Jew.

# 6

## MARION MILL PREMINGER

My final production at the Josefstadt was *The First Legion,* an American play by Emmet Lavery. It was set in a monastery and had a large all-male cast. As a tribute to me, many of Austria's and Germany's leading actors accepted minor roles in order to be part of my farewell. We opened on October 8, 1935. Because of the religious theme, Cardinal Innitzer, who later collaborated with the Nazis, was in attendance. So was the new Chancellor, Kurt von Schuschnigg, who usually kept out of public view for fear of being assassinated like his predecessor Engelbert Dollfuss. In fact, we received a threat that a bomb would explode during the performance. When the cream of Viennese society arrived at the theatre, everyone was searched by grim-faced, heavily armed police.

*The First Legion* was one of the most successful plays ever presented in Vienna and had one of the longest runs in theatrical history there. At the end the audience gave me a standing ovation.

But my bags were packed. I left Vienna three days later. My parents and many of my friends were at the station to see me off. I was bound for Paris and then for Le Havre, where I was to board the *Normandie* for America. A dream was coming true.

The last figure I saw on the platform was my young wife

Marion. She wanted to spend a few weeks with her family in Hungary before joining me. Though I loved her dearly I thought the short separation might be a pleasant change.

I met Marion in 1931. She came to my office at the Josefstadt to ask me for some legal advice which was rather odd because I had never practiced law for one minute after obtaining my degree. She was a dancer-performer in a night-club revue and was having a contract dispute with the management. A friend had told her that I was the man to straighten out her problems.

She was tall, dark, and beautiful, with an elegance about her. I had known a number of women but no one captivated me as Marion did from the first day I saw her. We were married in Town Hall on August 3, 1932, her birthday.

I asked her to give up the stage. She agreed at once. She had a condition of her own: she did not want any children, at least not for a long time. I hoped she would eventually change her mind because I don't believe there is much point in marrying unless you have children.

Though I was completely charmed by Marion I soon noticed that most of what she told people about her past, her family, her background was pure fantasy. She was possessed by a spirit of wishfulness that converted the modest home in which she was born into a castle and her middle-class family into rich nobility. Her name was Deutsch but she claimed to be a Baroness Deuth, using Mill as her stage name because her family did not want their aristocratic friends to know that she was an actress. She told her stories so often and with such conviction that she eventually believed them herself.

She continued to apply her imagination to our life together. In her autobiography, *All I Want Is Everything*, she describes in great detail the house we had in California. Not a single room or piece of furniture is recognizable. She speaks of white carpets. They did not exist. She says we had twenty telephones. We had four. She describes a painting by Renoir hanging over the piano. We had a piano but never owned a Renoir. But if Marion were alive today she would argue that we did.

She joined me in Hollywood soon after I arrived, just missing by a few days the party Joseph Schenck had given in my honor. That tardiness bothered her only briefly. Soon she imagined that she had attended the party. She invented stories of the famous people she met and what they were wearing, and what fun it was. Soon she developed a passion for parties. They were perhaps a substitute for the theatrical career she had given up. They assumed for her the same importance that a performance has for an actor. I did not feel the way she did. I was getting up early in the morning, working at the studio all day, and was bored by the phoniness of most of the people who delighted her. We began to go our separate ways, though we did not notice it for a while.

# 7

## DOWN AND UP IN NEW YORK

Though she hated to leave Hollywood and the parties, Marion did not complain when my contract with Twentieth Century-Fox expired at the end of 1937. She packed our belongings and we moved to New York.

We settled in the St. Regis Hotel. It did not occur to me to try a more modest style of living. While I consider it unprofessional to waste money on my stage and film productions—and I usually complete them on or under budget—I enjoy luxury in my private life. I contacted some of the people I had met during the *Libel!* rehearsals and introduced Marion to them. That resulted in many parties and late nights at El Morocco. Our California savings dwindled away. During the day I looked for work as director or for plays to produce and people to back me. The results were negative.

On March 12, 1938, Hitler invaded Austria. My parents, my brother and his family were in Vienna. Although I pleaded with overseas operators for forty-eight hours I could not reach them. I tried to telephone their friends. I could not contact those who were Jewish. The others refused to take my call. Two days later my parents called me from Switzerland. As soon as they had learned of the Nazi invasion they managed to get seats on the first train leaving Vienna for Italy. It was too late. The Germans already had sealed the border and the train was turned back. My father appealed for help to an old friend, the Chief of Police in Vienna, Otto Skubl. At great risk to himself, he put my parents on a plane to Zürich. My brother Ingo, his wife and daughter escaped across the border to Czechoslovakia and later joined my parents in Switzerland.

The next step was to get them all out of Europe. When they had visited me the summer before in California I suggested that they apply for immigration visas to the United States, because it seemed obvious to me that the Nazis would sooner or later move into Austria. My father refused. He was convinced that I was mistaken and felt it was wrong and unpatriotic for a prominent Austrian to show such lack of confidence in the future of his country. He misjudged the situation because he was too close to it. Now the quota for immigrants had been filled. My family could obtain visitor visas only. A few weeks later we all embraced on a New York pier. But this was only a temporary solution. They had to leave the country when their visas expired. There seemed to be nothing anybody could do about it.

One day Tallulah Bankhead called me. We knew each other only slightly, having met a few times at parties and at the Stork Club. She asked me to meet with her father, who was Speaker of the House of Representatives, and her uncle, who was a Senator, at her father's office in Washington the next morning at eleven o'clock. They would discuss my family's problem with me.

I met with the two Southern gentlemen and they told me that they were ready to introduce a special bill which would permit my parents and my brother and his family to become Americans regardless of the quota. A few weeks later they went to Canada for a day, applied for their visas, and returned as immigrants. When I went to see Tallulah and expressed my thanks she drawled, "Oh it's nothing, daaahling!"

By that time my money was very low. I had not paid the hotel bill for several weeks. Colonel Serge Obolensky, who was then the manager of the St. Regis, came to see me. "Don't worry," he said. "The hotel is less than half full. You can stay as long as you want to. I know you will pay eventually. But," he added, "please, don't use room service." I am forever grateful to Serge.

Eventually, as he predicted, I paid my debt to the St. Regis in full.

My father had a modest amount of money, some of it from a Swiss bank account he had maintained and some of it derived from the sale of jewels my mother had managed to hide on her body during the flight from Vienna. He became aware of my difficulties and offered help. He wanted to purchase a farm where he, my mother, my brother Ingo, Ingo's wife Kate and their daughter Eva, Marion and I could live in rural comfort for the rest of our lives.

I thanked him but I said, "I'm not a farmer. Please don't worry about me. Things aren't going too well for me at the moment but I believe in my future."

To my surprise Lee Shubert, the head of the Shubert empire, offered me an office in the Sardi building rent free. In return, he asked only for first call on any production I would undertake.

I could not afford a secretary but I met Jean Rodney, the stage-struck daughter of a wealthy Wall Street broker who wanted to learn about the theatre. She volunteered to work for me without pay in order to observe the activities of a producer-director.

There wasn't much for her to observe in the beginning. I put in a full working day trying to find a play to produce or a producer to hire me. Meanwhile Jean and a friend of hers raised the money to put together a production company. They enlisted Bill Brady, who owned the Playhouse on Forty-eighth Street, and they decided to do a revival of Sutton Vane's *Outward Bound*. They asked me to direct it.

It is a play about a mismatched group of people on a boat who find themselves thrown together under circumstances they can't understand. They eventually discover that they are all dead and traveling outward into eternity.

I cast Laurette Taylor to play Mrs. Midgit, the key part. Laurette was then fifty-four years old. She had been an alcoholic for ten years, had started rehearsals on several plays but always dropped out, and this was to be yet another comeback attempt. She was a truly inspired actress who in her youth had married the playwright J. Hartley Manners. He wrote for her *Peg o' My*

*Heart,* which opened in 1912 on Broadway and ran for two years, breaking all records.

Laurette's tragic story is told in a book by her daughter Marguerite Courtney entitled *Laurette.* Apparently the actress had been drinking for years before Manners died in 1928, but with his death she disintegrated.

I had met her during one of the times she was trying to act again. Gilbert Miller had cast her in his production of *L'Espoir.* I visited one of the rehearsals. Afterward I met her in Gilbert's office. She kept up a stream of complaints about her leading man, Sir Cedric Hardwicke. "I can't act with that ham," she told Miller. "He's already looking out at the audience and there isn't a soul there yet. What do you think he'll be like when there are people out front?"

It was an obsession with her, that performers should look at one another. Eye contact was most important, she felt, and she was right.

One day she didn't turn up for rehearsal. When she stayed away for a whole week, Miller preferred charges to Actors Equity. The union suspended her for a year. She returned to the bottle.

Bill Brady called me into his office just before rehearsals of *Outward Bound* were to begin. He had resisted my casting of Laurette but I insisted and prevailed. "Believe me, she's a hopeless drunk. She'll never be able to remember her lines and eventually she won't show up and we'll have to get someone else. To save time I will have my wife sit in the balcony and watch rehearsals. When Laurette drops out, she'll step in."

Bill Brady's wife was Gladys George, a well-known actress. I was still convinced that Laurette was the one to play the role.

We began rehearsing. Gladys George sat inconspicuously in the dark balcony.

As we broke for lunch Laurette asked me to eat with her. We were seated at a table in a nearby restaurant and she opened the conversation by putting her script in front of me. "I saw that bitch in the balcony and I know what she's waiting for. Let's not delay things. Here's my script. She can have the part right now."

"Look, Laurette," I told her, "I will give you a script with all the changes and cuts that I plan to make. You take it home and learn your part. If it takes two days, fine. If it takes ten days, fine. I promise you that Gladys George will not rehearse in the meantime. Only your understudy will rehearse. You will play this part, and only you."

She was back in a few days, letter-perfect. The other members of the cast were still fighting to remember their lines and that made her feel secure. She stayed sober through the rehearsals and didn't waver during the critical days of stress before the opening.

When she made her entrance on opening night, December 22, 1938, the audience rose and gave her a ten-minute ovation. Many people wept. Richard Watts wrote in his review the next day: "It merely happens that Laurette Taylor is one of the finest actresses in the world."

Laurette had a rare gift of concentration. She always looked at the other actors even if it meant playing with her back to the audience. She never had to raise her voice. She was so much the character she acted that audiences were gathered in to her and could hear what she was saying even if she whispered. And she took direction beautifully. She put her faith in the director and followed his instructions without question.

She was impatient with other members of the cast when they looked at the audience while they were addressing her. Bramwell Fletcher had many scenes with her in *Outward Bound*. In rehearsal I compelled him to look at her but once the play began its long run of 255 performances he began to turn to the audience more and more. She warned him one day that if he did it one more time she would embarrass him so that he would never forget it. When he turned from her that night and spoke his lines out to the audience she began to stare at his fly. It is an actor's nightmare that he might be on stage with an unbuttoned or unzipped fly. Fletcher was aghast but didn't dare check it in front of the audience. He ad-libbed some excuse and went off stage. He found that there was nothing wrong but he was so shaken by the experience that he never let his attention drift again. When he was supposed to look at Laurette, he looked at her.

That season Laurette won an award for the best performance over such outstanding stars as Tallulah Bankhead, who was superb in *The Little Foxes*, Maurice Evans in *Hamlet*, Katharine

Hepburn in *The Philadelphia Story*, and Raymond Massey in *Abe Lincoln in Illinois*. She was even more excited when she learned that Eleanor Roosevelt had selected *Outward Bound* to play a command performance in the National Theatre in Washington on President Roosevelt's birthday, January 30.

It was done every year for the benefit of the March of Dimes, an organization raising funds to fight polio. The chosen show closed for a single night on Broadway to give a performance in Washington, with the President and leading politicians and diplomats in attendance.

Laurette could hardly contain herself. She was, like me, an admirer of Roosevelt. We were invited to have supper after the performance in the White House. For weeks Laurette collected thoughts on what she might ask him and comments she might make.

I was equally excited.

Tables of eight had been arranged. To our delight Laurette and I were seated at the one where the President's wheelchair had been placed. Laurette just stared at him, her face ashen and all the questions she had planned to ask forgotten. Roosevelt was aware of her petrified condition. To help her relax he began to complain laughingly about a certain duty of his office that every year spoiled his birthday for him.

"It's that son of a bitch Hitler," he explained, looking directly at Laurette. "My birthday is also the anniversary of his coming to power. He makes one of his speeches at the occasion and I, on my birthday, must listen to that crap."

His warmth and his deliberately informal language gradually eased Laurette's nervousness.

Of all the people I have met in my life the two who impressed me most were Franklin Roosevelt and Jawaharlal Nehru. Roosevelt's personality left an indelible memory. He had the gift to make you feel he cared about you and was truly interested in what you had to say. He conveyed the sense of trusting you, liking you. You felt he would remain your friend for life.

Nehru had that same quality. I met him when I was in New Delhi researching a film I hoped to produce about the life of Mahatma Gandhi. I asked for an audience with Nehru, who was Prime Minister at the time. He was extremely busy and two weeks went by before I got an appointment. As I was ushered in I was told that he could spare me only a few minutes. But once I faced him across his desk he appeared to have nothing on his mind but my film. He talked about Gandhi and then about films in general. He took me into a projection room in the same building where he sometimes viewed films. But he felt he could enjoy them better and do them more justice if he saw them in a theatre as part of an audience. The visit lasted more than two hours. His attitude of genuine interest and concern gave me the feeling that I had acquired a new friend.

Laurette Taylor finished a long run in *Outward Bound* without missing a performance. She then accepted the lead in *The Glass Menagerie,* written by a young playwright, Tennessee Williams. It opened in Chicago to brilliant reviews but no one came to see it.

Laurette telephoned me in great distress. "I don't understand it," she said. "I feel it is a marvelous play but we have no audiences and we're running out of money. I'm afraid we'll have to close it." I told her I was going to California and would stop over in Chicago and see it. So I did. Her performance was beautiful. I hurried backstage to her dressing room. "You are terrific! The play is wonderful!" I shouted in my enthusiasm. "You must bring it to New York. It will be a tremendous hit."

When I left her a little man stopped me just outside her door. He asked if he had heard right. Did I really believe it would be a hit in New York? I told him vehemently that I did.

He was a lawyer from New York representing the new owner of the Forty-eighth Street Playhouse. After his conversation with me he contacted his clients, who put up enough money so that Eddie Dowling, who was the producer-director-actor of *The Glass Menagerie,* could bring the play to New York. It was a sensational success.

# 8

## MY DEAR BARRYMORE

Though *Outward Bound* was a hit, it did not contribute much toward improving my personal finances. However, a few weeks after the opening Cheryl Crawford, a Broadway producer, came to my office and offered me $1,500 to direct a play for her. The play's title was *Yankee Fable,* the author was Lewis Meltzer, and the star Ina Claire, a great favorite of New York audiences and critics. The rehearsals went well and we opened a two week pre-Broadway engagement in Boston. Ina Claire could not remember her lines. She had known them to perfection during rehearsals. After the opening I walked with her every day for hours in the Boston Common while she recited her part over and over without a single mistake. But when the curtain went up she could not concentrate. I was sorry for her because she was a very good actress and tried very hard. We had no choice but to close the play.

Because of my success with *Outward Bound* I was approached by Richard Aldrich, who was running a summer theatre in New England: the Cape Cod Playhouse. He and Richard Myers were forming a partnership to produce plays on Broadway with the backing of John Hay (Jock) Whitney. I joined them. During our association I never asked for credit as producer. But I acted as producer and I received a producer's cut, one third, in addition to my full share as director. Our first play was *My Dear Children,* a comedy by Catherine Turney and Jerry Horwin. It was not a good play but we saw in it a vehicle for John Barrymore's return to the stage. He had wrecked his health with heavy drinking and needed money to pay his debts. I went to California to see him and he agreed to do the part on condition that one of his three daughters be played by his young wife Elaine Barrie, a woman of little acting ability. I cast a gifted newcomer, Dorothy McGuire, as another of the daughters.

To capitalize on public curiosity to see the unpredictable, brilliant, drunken Barrymore in person we planned a long out-of-town tour before the New York opening. It was launched in Princeton with big success. People stood and cheered, delighted with Barrymore's broad mockery of himself.

He made a curtain speech in which he first thanked me, then went through the cast thanking each player and finally naming every electrician and stagehand. He had an excellent memory when he chose to exercise it. At the end he started to leave the stage without mentioning Aldrich and Myers. Almost to the wings he stopped and came back to the footlights. "I almost forgot," he said, pretending to be flustered. "I almost forgot to thank my producers, my, ah producers . . . let me see, ah, what *are* their names? Has someone got a program? Yes, yes here it is, Richard Aldrich and Richard, ah, Myers."

The audience thought it was hilarious but Aldrich and Myers were not amused. They both were able men but they were unfortunately somewhat afraid of Barrymore and it gave him perverse pleasure to torment people who were intimidated by him.

Several months later *My Dear Children* was still touring somewhere in the Midwest when I received an urgent telephone call from Myers, who was shepherding the production. He said that Barrymore had a fight with Elaine Barrie, was going to divorce her, and wanted her fired from the company at once. Myers begged me to fly out immediately and see what could be done. Barrymore had requested that I bring with me his close friend, the playwright Charles MacArthur.

MacArthur was married to Helen Hayes and they lived in the country, but he happened to be in New York staying at the

Gotham Hotel. I arranged to call for him early the following morning.

When I arrived at the Gotham, MacArthur greeted me, soaking wet. There was an anxious young man with him. "What happened?" I asked. He was cheerful. "I didn't want to oversleep," he explained, "so I asked this young man to stay with me and wake me up by pouring cold water on me. And he did." Apparently he had slept in his clothes.

In the taxi on the way to the airport he produced two bottles of Scotch he had purchased for the journey. At that time airplanes did not serve alcoholic beverages nor did they permit passengers to drink on board. Charles kept disappearing into the toilet, emerging each time in an increasingly benign mood.

When we arrived at our destination Barrymore was waiting for us at the airport, accompanied by the big male nurse we had hired to keep him from drinking. Each of them had a bottle sticking out of his coat pocket.

That night I sat through the performance of *My Dear Children* and was horrified. Barrymore delivered lines of his own invention, unconcerned by either the plot or the other actors. Most of the time he sat, sagging, on a bench placed center stage. He remained there whether he was supposed to be on stage or not, sometimes seeming to fall asleep.

Obviously the audience didn't mind. They had come to see him play a drunken clown and he was obliging them. It lasted approximately forever.

I said nothing as I went with the cast to the train that was taking us to the next stop, St. Louis. We boarded the special car on which the company traveled and I joined Barrymore in his compartment. The male nurse and Charles MacArthur crowded in with us and we opened the discussion about Elaine Barrie.

Barrymore was astonished when his friend MacArthur defended Elaine. He had invited him because he expected his support. "You shouldn't throw her out," MacArthur kept repeating, throughout a long, sentimental speech about gentlemanly behavior. "Even if you don't love her any more, you shouldn't mistreat a lady."

The male nurse hated Elaine. An enormous man of six feet six, he could not contain himself. He said to MacArthur, "If you say

one more word I'll push you under the bunk." The bunk was
about five inches from the floor.

I announced that we all needed sleep and went to my Pullman
section. I was almost asleep. Suddenly the curtain was pulled
aside and two women in dressing gowns crawled in and sat on
my chest. One was Elaine Barrie and the other was her mother,
Mrs. Jacob.

Mrs. Jacob began to curse Barrymore in coarse, abusive language. She threatened that if I dared take her daughter out of
the play she would tell the press on arrival in St. Louis that Barrymore had tried to rape her, his own mother-in-law. Several
times. In fact, as recently as yesterday. I said ungallantly, "Who
would believe you, Mrs. Jacob?" She ignored it. "If my daughter
doesn't stay in the cast I will destroy Barrymore!" she cried,
shaking a fist. It had been a long day. In no uncertain terms I
asked them to get off my chest and leave.

There was no mention of rape the next day. We reached a
polite compromise. Elaine Barrie would remain in the part for
another week, during which I would find and rehearse a replacement. Barrymore agreed to the delay and Elaine Barrie accepted
dismissal, but we had to pay her full salary for the run of the
play.

That night Barrymore's performance was even more appalling
than it had been the night before. His excesses took so much
time that the curtain didn't come down until one in the morning.

The whole cast gathered afterward in the hotel restaurant to
have something to eat. I kept very silent, which provoked Barrymore to ask, "Well, Professor"—he always called me that—
"how did you find our performance?" "In one word: abomina-
ble," was my answer. There was a hush. Everybody expected a
fight. Instead he said quietly, "Well, come tomorrow."

The next evening he did the part exactly as we had rehearsed
it, every line perfect, every bit of business impeccable. The play
ended at ten minutes to eleven as it was supposed to.

I went to his dressing room and said, "Jack, why can't you do
this every night?"

He grinned at me. "B-o-r-e-d, my dear boy, bored."

When he was sober he was brilliant and entertaining. Unfortunately, as happens with advanced alcoholics, it required only a few sips of a martini to get him drunk.

His stage deportment was at its worst in Chicago. He took up residence in a whorehouse, from which he emerged dirty and hung over. He occupied the bench at center stage throughout the performance, while the actors had to play around him. Often he was too tired to leave the bench during intermission. Sometimes he remained there half asleep between matinee and evening performances.

Just before the play was due to come to New York, Dorothy McGuire wrote me. She asked to be released from her contract. She said she couldn't bear seeing Barrymore make a fool of himself. It must have been a tough decision for a young actress to give up her Broadway debut in a good part opposite John Barrymore. I have undying respect for her integrity.

*My Dear Children* opened in New York on January 31, 1940. It was sold out for ten months in advance.

After the opening Jock Whitney gave a small dinner party at his house for the producers and a few friends. When it was over I went to the Monte Carlo night club where the cast was celebrating. As I was walking through the overcrowded room toward the long table where Barrymore and the other actors were sitting, a figure stood up in my path. It was Elaine Barrie. She said, "I'll come with you. I want to speak to Jack." I asked her, "Please, Elaine, don't. We have had enough trouble."

I couldn't stop her. She took a chair across the table from Jack. While everybody watched nervously, they talked in low voices. After about thirty minutes Barrymore got up, helped Elaine with her coat, and said good night to us. They left the night club together, encountering the usual group of reporters who followed Barrymore around. They asked him where he was going. He answered: "For a change, gentlemen, I'm going home to sleep with my wife."

At the next performance Elaine Barrie was back in the cast and her replacement, Doris Dudley, had to be dropped. A few months later Barrymore got tired of the play and quit despite a big advance sale.

Two years later he was dead.

# 9

## MARGIN FOR ERROR

While *My Dear Children* was on the road an agent offered me a play that I liked, *Margin for Error* by Clare Boothe. My partners Aldrich and Myers agreed with me. I met Clare Boothe and told her we wanted to produce her play but the script needed work. She was agreeable about the changes I wanted and we decided to meet daily about noon in my rooms at the St. Regis and work together.

On our first day the telephone rang at six-thirty. A voice said: "This is Henry Luce. I am downstairs. May I come up and have dinner with you and my wife?"

He came up and we ate. Throughout the meal he said scarcely a word but never took his eyes off her. He obviously was very much in love with Clare. He joined us for dinner every evening during the several weeks we worked on the changes.

We began rehearsals. The cast of *Margin for Error* included Sam Levene, Bramwell Fletcher, Leif Erickson, and, in the role of Karl Baumer, the villainous Nazi consul, Rudolf Forster, a well-known German actor. One day when I arrived for rehearsal the stage doorman delivered a note to me which Forster had left with him. It read: "Dear Otto, I'm going home to rejoin Adolf. Love, Rudolf."

Our out-of-town opening was only a couple of weeks away. I

auditioned actor after actor for the role, but there was no one suitable. There seemed to be a shortage of Nazis in New York at the time. Finally, Clare Boothe suggested that I play the part. I had not acted since I was nineteen and acting didn't interest me any more. I told Clare that I would play the part on the road, but if the audiences and critics in Princeton and Washington did not like my performance we would have to find someone else before we opened in New York.

To obtain the physical effect I wanted I played the Nazi consul with a monocle, a saber scar on my cheek, and a clean-shaven head.

Albert Einstein attended the opening in Princeton. My wife Marion sat next to him. At the end she asked him, "Well, how did you like Otto?" Einstein was a gentle, unassuming man who, away from his work, gave the impression of being slightly confused. He peered at her. "Who?" he asked. "My husband Otto." "Oh, he was good," said Einstein, "very good indeed. But you know, the actor who impressed me the most was the one who played the consul."

*Margin for Error* opened in Washington to mixed notices. However, there was unanimous praise for my performance and I decided to continue in the part. My chief concern was to repair the script before the New York opening. The second act, particularly, was in trouble. Clare Boothe, however, was no longer in a cooperative mood. We postponed the opening and closed the play for a week. We were all ready and willing to work around the clock. All of us except her. She usually arrived at the theatre around eight in full evening dress bound for some party, dropped off the few pages she had rewritten during the day, and left. I lost my temper several times and told her what I thought of her unprofessional arrogant behavior. But she had apparently given up on her play.

I was also having trouble with Sam Levene during this last week of rehearsals. He played the biggest and most important part of the play, a Jewish policeman. Since my personal success as actor he developed—perhaps unconsciously—a certain hostility against me as director. If I said, for instance, "Please get up on this speech and cross over to the left," he would object and say, "No, I prefer to get up on the next speech." I did not want to waste precious time and gave in wherever possible. So I usually answered, "All right, do it your way if it makes you happy." However, I used the phrase "If it makes you happy" so often that it began to irritate him. One day he exploded. "Mr. Preminger," he cried, "I was born unhappy, I grew up unhappy, I enjoy being unhappy, and I am not going to be happy because you tell me to." I was amused and laughed. After a moment he did too. We became good friends.

*Margin for Error* opened on Broadway at the Plymouth Theatre on the third of November, 1939. It was a hit and ran for 264 performances. Walter Winchell loved the play and plugged it in his influential column almost daily. Henry Luce's *Life* magazine published a big spread with many photographs of scenes from the production. I appeared in several of them. The captions identified all members of the cast by their names except me. I was referred to only as the consul. Clare's revenge. I could not care less.

Despite my heavy schedule I accepted an invitation to teach at the Yale Drama School three times a week. I commuted to New Haven in my small car. There were some very talented young people in my classes, among them Fred Coe, who became a stage and television producer and director of great distinction and Harry Kleiner, whom I signed later to write several screenplays for me in Hollywood.

*Margin for Error* did so well that my partners and I decided to send a second company out on the road. Again the part of the German consul was difficult to cast. Kurt Katsch, the very talented actor whom I had met during my engagement at the theatre in Zürich fifteen years earlier, had arrived in New York with a group of refugees and came to see me. He needed work but could not speak English. I invited him to see a performance of *Margin for Error*. Afterward in my dressing room I asked him if he wanted to play my part in the touring company. He was at first flabbergasted but grew enthusiastic when I revealed my plan. I was going to write out every line for him phonetically. Then he was to attend every performance until the road tour began. He learned to imitate me in every detail. He shaved his head and adopted the monocle and the scar. He knew the lines by heart but had only a vague idea what they meant. He received very good notices and at the end of the tour had even learned some English. It is ironic that two refugees from Hitler made a success playing a violent Nazi.

Katharine Hepburn was appearing in *The Philadelphia Story* at the Shubert Theatre across the street from the Plymouth where I played *Margin for Error*. Sometimes we went out for supper together after the theatre. One night we sat in the upstairs dining room at "21" which was almost empty when Joseph Schenck came in with Herbert Bayard Swope, the former editor of the *World*. I had not seen Schenck since my fight with Zanuck and he acted as though he had forgotten that he refused even to accept my telephone calls. His face lit up when he saw us and he headed directly for our table.

"Otto! I'm so glad to see you," he said. "It's wonderful that you're such a great success . . ." He turned to Katharine Hepburn and went on enthusiastically. "Miss Hepburn, I discovered this man. I saw his brilliant productions in Vienna and brought him to America."

He drew a breath and, smiling at her, said, "You know, Miss Hepburn, I often wonder how come that during all these years in Hollywood we two never met."

Hepburn responded in her clipped manner, emphasizing every word. "Mr. Schenck, I consider that one of my most gratifying achievements."

But nothing could deter Schenck. He waved to Swope to join him, sat down at our table and ordered his dinner.

Jack Haley, Ann Sothern, Otto Preminger, Mary Boland, and Edward Everett Horton, *Danger, Love at Work*, 1937

Otto shows Elaine Barrie how to be spanked by John Barrymore, *My Dear Children*, 1939 ( UNITED PRESS INTERNATIONAL )

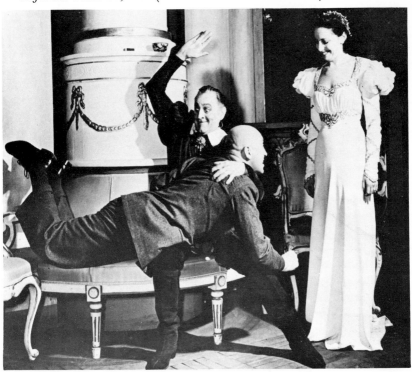

Otto and Joan Bennett (*Margin for Error* © 1943 TWENTIETH CENTURY-FOX FILM CORPORATION. COURTESY OF TWENTIETH CENTURY-FOX)

Milton Berle discusses a story point with Otto while the makeup man shaves Otto's head (*Margin for Error* © 1943 TWENTIETH CENTURY-FOX FILM CORPORATION. COURTESY OF TWENTIETH CENTURY-FOX)

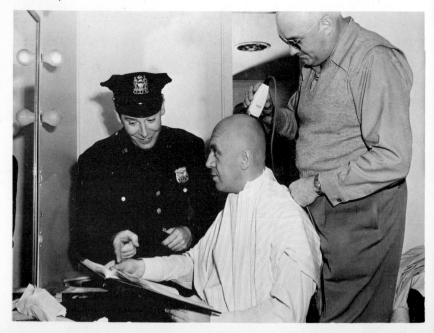

Clifton Webb, Otto, Gene Tierney, and Dana Andrews (*Laura* ©
1944 TWENTIETH CENTURY-FOX FILM CORPORATION. COURTESY OF
TWENTIETH CENTURY-FOX)

Clifton Webb, Gene Tierney, Kathleen Howard, and Dana Andrews (*Laura* © 1944 TWENTIETH CENTURY-FOX FILM CORPORATION. COURTESY OF TWENTIETH CENTURY-FOX)

Dana Andrews, Otto, and Alice Faye. Cameraman Joe La Shelle behind Otto (*Fallen Angel* © 1945 TWENTIETH CENTURY-FOX FILM CORPORATION. COURTESY OF TWENTIETH CENTURY-FOX)

# 10

## LADY ON A SWING

I met Moss Hart soon after my arrival in New York. I liked him right away and grew fonder of him the better I knew him. Moss was a gentle and shy man. He knew great poverty before he wrote, with George Kaufman, *Once in a Lifetime* and became, overnight, famous and rich.

Success had a tragic effect on Moss. He suffered from severe depressions with suicidal tendencies. He told me that he used to tie himself to his bed before he went to sleep at night to restrain himself from an impulsive suicide.

Psychoanalysis helped him very much. I did not believe in it as a science or cure, but Moss converted me. I told him once that I could not imagine myself going to the office of a stranger and telling him for hours the most intimate details of my life. His answer sounded convincing: "If you had no toothache could you imagine letting a stranger drill your teeth? You most likely don't need the help of a psychoanalyst." Maybe.

Because of his fear of being rejected he was particularly vulnerable in his relationship with women.

All his friends were very happy when he fell in love with Edith Atwater, a young actress who was in the cast of his play *The Man Who Came to Dinner*. After a lengthy courtship he asked her to marry him and she accepted. I was deeply shocked when he called me from Boston one day and told me that Edith had changed her mind and was going to marry someone else. He sounded desperate.

I called her and took her to Sardi's for lunch and pleaded with her not to break her engagement or, at least, postpone her decision and think it over for a while. I had arranged for her agent, Jane Broder, to join us. I have great respect for Jane, professionally and as a woman. Both of us talked to Edith Atwater for hours until we were the only guests left in the restaurant. But it was in vain. She married someone else and, as it happened, neither her marriage nor her career prospered.

Hart survived the blow with the help of his doctor, who also advised him that it would improve his self-confidence if he wrote a play by himself without the collaboration of Kaufman.

The result was *Lady in the Dark*. Moss wrote it originally as a straight play. But he felt perhaps still not secure enough and decided to make it a musical with the help of George and Ira Gershwin.

Moss invited me to attend the opening in Boston. We stood together in the back of the theatre. Gertrude Lawrence, the star of the show, was sitting on a swing when Danny Kaye entered. Kaye was, until then, a night-club performer. This was his stage debut. He had to sing a song especially written for him, and he did it brilliantly. The audience applauded and cheered until he repeated the song and then stood and cheered until he did it again. Gertrude Lawrence sat on the swing the whole time waiting for him to finish and to follow with her song, "Jenny," which, during rehearsals, was considered the hit of the play.

Moss whispered to me, "We'll have to move Gertie's song. It is not fair to have her follow Kaye." But Gertie had made her own plan while watching the long noisy ovation. She had rehearsed her number singing it on the swing with full voice. But now she decided that would not give much contrast to Kaye. So she waited through all his encores and the noisy applause until the audience was quiet. Then she got off the swing, walked slowly to the footlights, and whispered her song. After the bedlam that had preceded her, it was stunningly effective. The audience applauded and cheered her with even greater enthusiasm than

Danny Kaye. Thanks to Gertie's showmanship it was not necessary to move the number.

I met Gertrude Lawrence when she tried out a play at Richard Aldrich's Cape Cod Playhouse before taking it to Broadway. The play was a failure but a few weeks later, to everybody's surprise, she and Aldrich got married. Aldrich is an attractive but very conservative and serious man, while Gertie was very outspoken and bubbling over with a delightful sense of humor. I ran into her in New York about a week after their wedding. She said laughingly, "I bet you didn't expect me to marry that man." I was taken aback and protested. I told her I thought he was an admirable choice and hoped they would be very happy. "Happy or not," she shrugged, "it doesn't matter. I needed roots and he is a very firm root."

They were very happy together until she died.

Moss Hart married Kitty Carlisle, a singer who was willing to give up her career for him. This marriage was the best thing that happened in his life. She loved him and, even more important, she made him know that she loved him. She accomplished what no psychoanalyst could: she cured him of his fears and his self-doubt. Thank you, Kitty.

# 11

## BACK TO HOLLYWOOD
## BY THE SIDE DOOR

In the fall of 1941, I directed and produced with Norman Pincus a comedy by Frank Gabrielson and Irvin Pincus: *The More the Merrier*. It was not merry and closed after sixteen performances. Two months later I did an excellent play—this time without a partner—about Woodrow Wilson's efforts on behalf of world peace: *In Time to Come,* by Howard Koch and John Huston. We were in rehearsal on the Sunday morning Pearl Harbor was bombed. The play opened on December 28, 1941, to rave reviews. At the end of the season it was named one of the ten best plays. But it closed after only forty performances. Nobody was in the mood to see a play about peace when we had just entered World War II.

Soon after Pearl Harbor, Darryl Zanuck left Twentieth Century-Fox to join the Army and photograph the war. William Goetz, Zanuck's executive assistant, ran the studio in his absence.

Nunnally Johnson saw me on Broadway in *Margin for Error* and offered me a part in a film he wrote and was about to produce: *The Pied Piper*. Goetz didn't object, assuming that Zanuck's ban against me did not extend to acting.

I accepted, rented a furnished apartment near the studio, and did the part for Johnson in the spring of 1942.

I was about to return to New York when my agent, Charles

Feldman, called. Twentieth Century-Fox was about to film *Margin for Error* and they wanted me for the role of the consul that I had played on Broadway. He got the studio to pay me an unusually high salary and give me star billing.

I told him I would be happy to do the part but I was primarily a director, I had directed *Margin for Error* successfully in New York, I had directed the touring company, why couldn't I direct the film? Feldman said it was out of the question.

I went to see Goetz, who said the same thing. Then, on the spur of the moment, I made him a reckless offer. I would direct the film without pay, taking only my salary as an actor. If, at the end of one week, my work wasn't satisfactory he could replace me as director. I would continue as actor and cooperate fully with the new director.

Goetz said he'd think about it and telephone me his decision the next day by three in the afternoon.

My agent was shocked when he heard what I had done. He said, "You're mad. Goetz will never let you direct. Just take the money for the acting job and go back to New York. Besides, nobody should work for free."

The next day I sat by the telephone for hours. Finally the call came. Goetz said we had a deal.

I directed *Margin for Error* for the trial week, fighting to keep my nerves under control. Goetz saw the rushes every day but said nothing until the week was over. Then he called me into his office and told me I could continue. He offered me a contract as actor, director, and producer for seven years with the usual options.

I was not happy with the script of *Margin for Error*. I felt it needed work. The film's producer, Ralph Dietrich, a nice man with very little experience, did not agree with me. Besides, he explained, there was no provision in the budget for a writer. So I decided to spend my own money and hired a young writer, Sam Fuller, who happened to be in town on leave from the Army. He came to my apartment every evening after I had finished at the studio and we worked together. We rewrote my scenes with Milton Berle, who played the Jewish policeman, and changed many others. Dietrich didn't notice the difference.

After the war Fuller became a successful producer-director-writer.

# 12

## LAURA

The story department at the studio circulated books and plays that were possibilities for films. Directors and producers also received suggestions from agents or hunted material on their own.

Out of all scripts, books, and plays I read while directing *Margin for Error*, only two attracted me. One was called *Army Wives* and the other, a suspense story by Vera Caspary, was *Laura*. Goetz looked them over and said fine, go ahead.

Then Zanuck returned. He accused Goetz of treachery. He was incensed by some of the decisions Goetz had made in his absence, among them signing me as director. He suspected that Goetz was trying to take the studio away from him. It was a fight for power. Zanuck refused to set foot on the lot as long as Goetz was still there. In the meantime he conducted business from his beach house in Santa Monica and summoned producers and directors one by one to conferences there. Eventually it was my turn.

We had not spoken for six years since our argument in 1937 over the *Kidnapped* script.

A butler escorted me through the house to the garden where Zanuck was sitting in swimming trunks beside his pool. His back was to me. He glanced around briefly and then gave me the back of his head again. He picked up a piece of paper and said: "I see you are working on a few things. I don't think much of them except for one, *Laura*. I've read it and it isn't bad. You can produce it but as long as I am at Fox you will never direct. Goodbye." "Goodbye," I said to his back and left.

Zanuck's next move was to put *Laura* and me in the B-picture unit. The quickies were then under the supervision of Bryan Foy, a charming man known as Brynie, who had succeeded Sol Wurtzel. I first worked on the script with a writer, Jay Dratler, but the dialogue wasn't right. Foy gave me permission to hire the writing team of the poet Samuel Hoffenstein and Betty Reinhardt. Hoffenstein practically created the character of Waldo Lydecker for Clifton Webb. He was in the habit of overwriting, but after the scenes were edited his dialogue was brilliant.

When we finished the *Laura* script we had almost an entirely new plot. From the original book we retained only the gimmick of Laura first appearing to be the victim of a murder and afterward, when she returns, becoming the chief suspect. When Vera Caspary read the script she wasn't pleased.

"Why are you making a B picture of my novel?" she asked me.

I told her it would be an excellent film. She wasn't convinced.

In fact, no one liked the script but those of us who had worked on it. Brynie Foy called me into his office and gave me the bad news.

"David read the *Laura* script and says it's lousy," he informed me. Brynie didn't like to read. His assistant David did it for him.

"Look, Brynie," I said, appealing to him the only way I knew I could reach him, "David is making seventy-five dollars a week and I'm making fifteen hundred. He doesn't like it but I do. Maybe you'd better read it yourself and decide which one of us is right."

He promised he would. We met the next morning in the studio elevator. In front of about ten people he said flatly, "David's right. The script stinks."

I knew the script did not stink. I asked Foy to send it to Zanuck for his opinion.

He was incredulous. "Zanuck hates you," he said. "All you need is for him to read this lousy script. He'll fire you."

"I'll take the risk," I said. Foy had no choice but to send the script to Zanuck, who had won his fight with Goetz and was back at the studio.

Darryl called Foy and me to his office two days after he received the *Laura* script. "You don't like the script, Brynie?" "No." "Why?" asked Zanuck curtly. Foy stumbled through some nonsense. One of his arguments was: how could you have a police story without a single scene in a police station?

Zanuck glared at him. "The fact that it doesn't have a routine scene in a police station is exactly what I like about it. I'll take over the supervision of the picture."

That meant that *Laura* and I were promoted to the A-picture unit. Zanuck had not changed his mind about not allowing me to direct, however. He sent the script to one director after another. None of them wanted to do it. As the refusals mounted, Zanuck's position on the script became increasingly uncertain.

Meanwhile, I was occupied with casting the film. In my view the role of Waldo Lydecker was critical to the success of *Laura*. The audience should not realize that he was the villain. Zanuck wanted to cast Laird Cregar in the role but I argued that it would tip the plot because Cregar was established as a heavy. I wanted someone unknown to film audiences and I thought the Broadway actor Clifton Webb would be right for the part.

In fact, I had already approached Webb through my old friend Féfé, who represented him. The war had killed his New York night club and he had moved to Hollywood to become an agent. I talked to Webb backstage in the Biltmore Theatre in Los Angeles where he was starring in a production of Noël Coward's *Blithe Spirit*. I gave him the *Laura* script and asked him to read it.

Zanuck was negative when I suggested Webb. The head of the casting department, Rufus LeMaire, who was present, took his cue from the boss's attitude and said that he had seen a test Webb made for MGM. He said the man was impossible. "He doesn't walk, he flies," implying that he was effeminate.

"Let's look at the Metro test," I urged. "I'm sure that Webb is right for the part."

Zanuck instructed LeMaire to obtain the test. Days passed. LeMaire kept making excuses. Féfé asked Webb and we found out the reason. He had never made a test for Metro or anyone else.

Zanuck had again included me in the inner group that lunched with him in the executive dining room. There I confronted Rufus LeMaire.

"When is the test of Webb coming?" I asked him. "Definitely tomorrow," he replied.

"You are a liar," I said quietly. "Webb never made a test. He never faced a camera during the eighteen months he was under contract to MGM.

Zanuck was fair enough to allow me to test Webb. He said I could have Gene Tierney play opposite him to give Webb the best possible chance. Gene was cast in the title role. Zanuck had yielded to me and cast as the leading man Dana Andrews, a young Fox contract actor with only a few screen credits.

I went to Webb's dressing room with the good news. He refused to make the test.

"My dear boy," he said, "if your Mr. Zanuck wants to see if I can act let him come to the theatre. I don't know your Miss Tierney and I don't want to make a test with her."

Zanuck was equally immovable. "I don't want to see him on the stage playing Noël Coward," he told me angrily. "I want to see him on film playing the part of Waldo Lydecker."

I hit upon a daring plan. Without telling Zanuck, I took a film unit to the theatre where Webb was performing. When the audience was gone, Webb, standing on the empty stage, delivered his famous monologue from *Blithe Spirit*. It made a superior piece of film. My cameraman was Joe La Shelle, who wasn't a first cameraman yet but was the only one available.

The next part was tricky. I had to risk Zanuck's wrath. I confessed to him what I had done and asked him to look at the test. He was furious. But when the screening was over he behaved with the fairness that was part of his complicated nature. "You're a son of a bitch," he said, "but you're right. He's very good. You can have Clifton Webb."

Webb and Zanuck became close friends and Webb became a big star at Fox for many years.

Zanuck had at last obtained a director for *Laura:* Rouben Mamoulian. He didn't like the script any more than the others who had turned it down but he had no other jobs in sight and needed the money. Mamoulian could read Hollywood politics as astutely as anyone in the business and was aware that Zanuck

was not exactly fond of me. The situation, he felt, gave him unlimited freedom to ignore me. He went ahead changing sets
and costumes without consulting me. When he began to make
changes in the script, I put my foot down. Mamoulian remembered that Zanuck liked the script and gave in.

He began to shoot. He asked me not to come to the set. He
said I made him nervous. Zanuck was in New York. I looked at
the dailies in a state of shock. I had chosen a simple dressing
gown for Judith Anderson but Mamoulian, influenced perhaps
by association with the Medea role for which she was famous,
had dressed her in something flowing and Grecian. It was totally
wrong for a contemporary story and so were his sets.

The performances were appalling. Judith Anderson was over-
acting, Dana Andrews and Gene Tierney were amateurish,
and there was even something wrong with Clifton Webb's performance.

I went to Lew Schreiber, who had succeeded Goetz as Zanuck's chief assistant. I insisted that he airmail the rushes to Zanuck in New York. Zanuck reacted with a furious telegram and instructed Schreiber to show it to Mamoulian and me. He hated
Dana Andrews' performance. He called him "an agreeable
schoolboy" who was not tough enough for the role of the detective. He added: "I was afraid of this all along and this is why I
wanted John Hodiak but stupidly listened to Preminger."

He wanted everything shot over again except for Clifton
Webb's closeups. Now Zanuck barred me from the set and Mamoulian started again.

The second set of dailies were identical to the first, or maybe
worse. Zanuck saw them when he returned from New York. We
were at lunch the next day, the table crowded with producers
and the top Fox brass. Zanuck looked at me.

"What do you think?" he asked abruptly. "Shall I take Mamoulian off the picture?"

Without hesitation I said, "Yes."

As we were leaving the dining room Zanuck said in an
offhanded way, "Monday you can start directing *Laura*. From
scratch."

I began by throwing out Mamoulian's ridiculous costumes and
sets. I replaced his designer with someone I found in the Fox

wardrobe department, Bonnie Cashin. She had never before made a picture on her own. She is now a world-famous designer of women's fashions.

Lucien Ballard, the cameraman assigned to the picture, was behaving strangely. He ignored me completely. While we were getting ready to shoot he would read a paper and smoke a cigar as if he was a guest on the set. I discovered that he hoped I would kick him off the picture. He was engaged to Merle Oberon and wanted to do a film with her at Metro.

I fired him, for which he was grateful, but Zanuck wasn't so accommodating. He held him to his Fox contract and put him to work on the test stage, the lowest job available.

I replaced him with Joe La Shelle, who had made the Clifton Webb test, promoting him to first cameraman. He won an Academy Award for *Laura* and became one of Hollywood's most sought-after cameramen.

When I scrapped Mamoulian's sets, the portrait of Laura went with them. It is important to the plot to have a recognizable portrait of Laura at which Dana Andrews keeps staring in the early part of the film when she is believed dead. Mamoulian had his wife paint one, but portraits rarely photograph well so I devised a compromise. We had a photograph of Gene Tierney enlarged and smeared with oil paint to soften the outlines. It looked like a painting but was unmistakably Gene Tierney.

When I started to rehearse the cast, everyone except Clifton Webb was hostile. I learned later that Mamoulian had called each of them individually and warned them that I did not like their acting and intended to fire them. Judith Anderson was particularly chilly.

"Mr. Preminger," she declared imperiously, "I hear that you don't like the way I'm playing my part."

The set was still. It was a declaration of war.

"No, I don't like anything about it," I answered.

"All right," she snapped. "Then show me how to do it better."

To her surprise I did. I knew every line in the script and I showed her what I wanted word by word, step by step, gesture by gesture. She's a good actress and although she thought I was wrong she did it exactly as I had shown her. At the end I said, "Tomorrow come and see the rushes with me and you will see what I mean." The whole cast watched the rushes the next day and from that moment on they were all on my side.

I made the first rough cut of the picture and showed it to Zanuck in his projection room. The seating arrangement for these viewings was as follows: Zanuck sat in the first row with the director, in this case me, and the editor, in this case Louis Loeffler. Behind us were about a dozen of Zanuck's yes-men. They didn't pay much attention to the picture. They had developed the art of reading the back of Zanuck's neck to perfection. They were able to anticipate whether he liked the film or not and adjusted their reactions accordingly.

It took very little skill that night to judge Zanuck's mood. He didn't even ask for their opinions. He got up and said to me, "Well, we missed the boat on this one. Be in my office tomorrow at eleven." And he left the room.

The next day Zanuck handed me a handful of memos from his yes-men. As was to be expected, they were all negative. A couple of them suggested shelving the film and writing it off as a loss. But their ideas how to save it were even worse.

Zanuck had his own plan. He called in one of his secretaries and a writer who was under contract to Fox. Then he began to walk up and down with the obligatory cigar and polo mallet dictating an outline for a rewrite of the script. His theory was that the fault lay with the last fifteen minutes, which he wanted to replace. Half the film was told from Waldo Lydecker's point of view, the other half from the detective's. Now Zanuck wanted to add a third part narrated by Laura after her return which contradicted and negated everything that we saw before.

Somehow my face must have betrayed my reaction because suddenly he stopped and said coldly: "If you don't like it, I'll get another director." I said no, I would direct it. I hoped to save what I could.

When I handed the new script to the actors, they too found it ridiculous. I told them we had to do it nonetheless. In two weeks we had finished the added scenes.

The evening Zanuck looked at the new version the projection room was practically empty. The yes-men had given up on the film. There were only the editor and I sitting next to Zanuck in the front row and in the back two people: Walter Winchell and a young lady. Whenever Winchell came to Hollywood Zanuck put an office at his disposal. They were friends. Zanuck invited him to see the picture and then have supper with him. Unlike the yes-men, Winchell and his companion seemed to like the film. They laughed, particularly at Clifton Webb's lines and his delivery. Zanuck seemed amazed. He turned around several times and looked at them.

When the screening was over Winchell walked up to Zanuck and said in his staccato manner: "Big time! Big time! Congratulations, Darryl. Except for the ending. I didn't get it. Didn't get it."

Zanuck demonstrated his flexibility. He turned to me: "Would you like to put your old ending back?"

I said, "Yes." And thanked Winchell.

The critics did not receive *Laura* with much enthusiasm. It didn't matter because audiences made *Laura* a phenomenal success at the box office. In England alone it grossed more than the production cost. I received a new seven-year contract with an increase in salary. Joe Schenck wrote me a congratulatory letter and Zanuck began to ask me to his house in Palm Springs for weekends.

# 13

## LADY MENDL AND THE FBI SET

Marion and I settled happily in California as I began to work again for Twentieth Century-Fox.

With her faked aristocratic background and enthusiasm for titles, it was only natural that she was drawn into the glittering social circle that revolved in those wartime years around Lady Mendl.

Elsie de Wolfe had become wealthy as an interior decorator, with rich clients all over Europe. She filled countless baronial homes with overstuffed sofas and monstrous antiques. In Paris she presided over a salon where she gathered rich and famous people.

She married a man with a title but no money, Sir Charles Mendl. When the war started they came to America. They chose California because Lady Mendl loved movie stars. There she surrounded herself with an assortment of refugee Europeans of such right-wing leanings that I referred to them jokingly as "the FBI set." I was sure that some of them were Nazi agents.

Lady Mendl's circle included at one time or another some of the wealthiest people in the world. One of her friends was Paul-Louis Veiller, the founder of Air France. His hobby was collecting castles. Veiller bought a house in Versailles for Lady Mendl as a gift for her lifetime. After she died the ownership reverted to Veiller.

While the Mendls lived in Hollywood, my wife Marion and Lady Mendl saw each other or spoke at least on the telephone every day. We were invited to all the parties the Mendls gave, and they entertained frequently. I found the affairs boring. So did Sir Charles, whom I rather liked. He was a charming and irreverent companion who entertained me with stories of his past.

Once, during the time he was a young attaché at the British Embassy in Paris, he was invited to dinner by a wealthy but dull man and sent his regrets. A friend protested. How could he pass up an opportunity to dine with one of the richest men in Paris? Sir Charles answered: "Sorry, I didn't know he would put a five-hundred-pound note under my plate. Next time I will accept."

Usually the Mendl parties were divided in two parts. The more desirable guests were asked to dinner, the less important after dinner. One night I saw Jules Stein, who was arriving with the second wave. He started as an eye doctor in Chicago, then became an agent for orchestras, and eventually developed MCA, the biggest theatrical and film agency in the world. It now owns, among other things, Universal Studios. Though the Mendl parties were strictly black tie, Stein was wearing a business suit. "Jules," I said, "where is your dinner jacket?" "No dinner," he replied, "no dinner jacket."

The other notable Hollywood hostesses of the period were Mrs. Gary Cooper and Mrs. Henry Hathaway. They invented high society in Hollywood according to their own rules. According to these rules, producers were never invited, nor writers, except those with international reputations. The group was restricted to actors, studio heads, and directors.

Marion took a passionate interest in these events and returned our social obligations with imaginative flair. At each party she changed the color of the table cloths and napkins. Green leaves served as place cards, with the names written in white ink.

She made a career of parties, which not only bored me but also conflicted with my need to rise early in the morning and go to work. We had many arguments about it before we reached an agreement. She would go out as much as she pleased and I would sometimes accompany her and sometimes not. Sometimes I would escort her to a party and then leave, sometimes call for her when the party was over.

It seemed to both of us a sensible arrangement. She did not object to my seeing other women. The only thing that she wanted to avoid at any price was divorce.

We lived like this for some time. Marion went with some friends on a trip to South America and Mexico. One day the telephone rang. It was my lawyer friend Sol Rosenblatt calling from Mexico City, where he was visiting a client. "Otto," he said, "prepare yourself for a surprise. I am calling for Marion. She wants a divorce. She met Axel Wennergren here, one of the world's richest men. They fell in love at first sight and want to get married as soon as he and she are divorced." I said, "All right," and he gave me instructions to go to the Mexican consul in Los Angeles who would have the divorce papers ready for me to sign.

Two days later I received a letter from Marion full of affectionate Hungarian farewells. She would never forget our happy years together but she knew that I did not love her any more and there was a man who loved her very much. She didn't want anything from me except a few personal belongings that would be picked up in a few days by her fiancé's private plane. I went downtown and signed all the necessary documents. The private plane did not arrive, but a few weeks later when I came home from the studio Marion was back. Mrs. Wennergren had refused to divorce her husband. She even followed Marion one day to the post office and shot at her. Luckily she missed. Whether the shooting really happened or was just a figment of Marion's Hungarian imagination I don't know. But now I insisted on the divorce. This time she wanted more than a few personal belongings. She got the best lawyers and they got for her all they could, according to California law. It was expensive but it felt good to be free.

Marion went to Africa and became a devoted follower of Albert Schweitzer. Eventually she came back and married a very wealthy man. In the beginning we were friendly when we ran into each other. But when I married again she stopped talking to me. However, she continued to use the name Preminger. As she lived only three blocks away from us, we kept receiving packages from various shops and department stores which were meant for her. That caused a great deal of inconvenience because we had to repack and return them. Finally I called her secretary and told her that I had no objection to her using my name but could she please add her husband's name so the stores would know for which Mrs. Preminger the packages were meant. The secretary's reaction was amazing. "You should be ashamed of yourself," she said furiously. "Do you know of whom you are speaking? You are speaking of a saint!" And so forth and so on. I couldn't do anything but hang up.

All in all, Marion always meant well. She was a decent human being without any malice. I felt very sad when I learned of her death last year.

# 14

## TALLULAH AND THE LUBITSCH TOUCH

One of the items of business left over from Bill Goetz's reign at Fox was the script *Army Wives*. He had assigned me to produce and direct it before Zanuck returned. I finished it quickly in the B-picture unit and it was released in 1944 at almost the same time as *Laura*. We gave it a new title: *In the Meantime, Darling*.

While I'm working on a film I am totally immersed in it and think of little else. When I see it at a preview for the first time with an audience a new, exciting element is added that often causes radical changes. Dialogue that seemed good during the long process of cutting and editing is suddenly not effective, and scenes that did not seem to work too well go over beautifully. After that I detach myself from the completed picture and concentrate on my next project. My memory starts to rid itself of the lines I knew glibly, and the images that were sharp in my mind fade away.

According to Freud, the ability to forget is the sign of a healthy mind. It also gives me the advantage that bad reviews don't trouble me. By the time they appear I am not vulnerable any more and can judge the critical opinions objectively, as though they concerned somebody else's work.

*In the Meantime, Darling* is one of my pictures I have forgotten. However, I recall one incident that occurred during the filming. It involved the actor Eugene Pallette, who was an admirer of Hitler and convinced that Germany would win the war.

The scene took place in a kitchen where Pallette and a black actor were to have a conversation. The black actor was seated at a table and I told Pallette to make his entrance and then to sit down beside him.

"You're out of your mind," he said. "I won't sit next to a nigger."

I went to Zanuck and had him fired. Most of his scenes had been shot. We wrote him out of what was left.

Shortly after that picture was finished, Ernst Lubitsch asked me to direct *A Royal Scandal* for him. He was recovering from a heart attack and for a while had to restrict himself to producing. I was his choice to direct *A Royal Scandal*. Zanuck agreed.

I hadn't known Lubitsch in Europe but we became friends in Hollywood. Since our homes in Bel Air were only a few minutes apart, we saw each other often.

We also used to meet at the regular Sunday afternoon coffee parties in the home of Walter Reisch, an Austrian writer who did the script for Lubitsch's *Ninotchka* with Billy Wilder. One Sunday afternoon Billy announced that I was really Martin Bormann in elevated shoes, with a face lift done by a blindfolded plastic surgeon in Luxemburg.

The script for *A Royal Scandal* was typically Lubitsch, full of hilarious scenes. We worked together on the casting and assembled a distinguished group that included Vincent Price, Charles Coburn, Anne Baxter, Mischa Auer, Eva Gabor, and, as Catherine the Second of Russia, Tallulah Bankhead.

The costumes were magnificent. Tallulah's skirts were so wide she couldn't get into her trailer dressing room. We had to build a special tent for her on the stage next to the set.

One day, just as we were beginning to rehearse, Lubitsch came to my office in a state of great excitement.

"Otto, I have wonderful news!" he said. "I had dinner last night with Garbo. I told her our story and she wants to play the part of Catherine."

"But, Ernst," I protested, "what about Tallulah?"

"Forget Tallulah," he said impatiently. "We'll pay her off. *We can get Garbo!*"

I said, "Ernst, stop, please STOP!" I told him how Tallulah rescued my family when they were facing deportation. I could never participate in anything that would hurt her. If Tallulah was removed from the picture I would resign too.

Lubitsch refused to listen to me. He insisted there would be some way to get around the situation. He took me to see Zanuck.

He was shouting as we walked through the door of Zanuck's office. "Darryl! We have *Garbo* for the picture!"

Garbo was indeed a magic name. She had retired from films a few years before, announcing she would never make another picture. Her passion for privacy was extreme. She went to such lengths to protect it that she appeared remote and cold.

When she first came to America as a young actress and started to make a great deal of money she gave it to a very rich, successful businessman, the Swedish match king, Ivar Kreuger, to invest for her. But his fortune and her savings were wiped out together. He committed suicide and she became fanatically frugal, determined never to be broke again.

I went to her house a few times. It was large and almost empty. The furniture consisted of a few chairs and some very good modern paintings in the living room and a bed and more paintings in the bedroom.

All Garbo's films were successful until she starred in the *Two-Faced Woman*, produced by Max Reinhardt's son Gottfried, which was a miserable failure. She retired in 1941 and has consistently turned down all offers to return to the screen.

When Lubitsch told Zanuck that Garbo had volunteered to play Catherine the Great, Darryl showed no excitement.

"I don't know that I prefer her to Tallulah," he said. He was using the standard yardstick of Hollywood: how successful was your last picture? Garbo's *Two-Faced Woman* had made no money, while Tallulah had just appeared in Alfred Hitchcock's *Lifeboat*, a box office winner.

Zanuck called the president of Twentieth Century-Fox in New York. Without hesitation the answer came back: Tallulah was far better than Garbo on the profit end of the business.

Lubitsch was so bitter over the rejection of Garbo that he took it out on Tallulah. He behaved rudely whenever he met her. He saw the dailies before me, since I was working on the set until late in the afternoon. One day I returned from lunch to find Tallulah stretched out on the floor of her tent sobbing with rage. Her costume was torn and thrown in a corner. She told me that Lubitsch had been there after seeing the dailies. He accused her of stealing a scene from Anne Baxter, who had only a small part in the picture. He said that Tallulah deliberately distracted the viewer's attention by closing her eyes while Anne was speaking.

It is unethical to distract the audience while another performer is speaking, and particularly low to do this to a newcomer. Tallulah would never behave like that. She was offended to the point of fury.

"I'm going to quit!" she told me, adding a number of unprintable comments about Lubitsch which she obviously had also made during their encounter. "I'm going straight to Zanuck. I'll give him back his $100,000 and leave."

I tried to calm her. I reminded her that Lubitsch was a sick man. I told her that I would inform him that I had directed her to close her eyes in that scene, which was a fact. When Lubitsch heard that he became calmer. I went back to Tallulah and informed her that Lubitsch was sorry. I asked her to come with me to his office and make up with him. She was a generous woman. She not only went with me, she even made apologies for what she had said while she was angry.

Tallulah enjoyed shocking people. Once I was sitting in the Stork Club with Marlene Dietrich and a few other friends when Tallulah came in.

"Otto, daaaahling!" she cried. "I haven't seen you in a long time. Do you want to admire my new breasts?" And she unbuttoned her dress, displaying her bosom. "I've just had them done. Aren't they marvelous?"

I was present when Tallulah delivered a speech that has become legendary. She had been pursued for a long time by a very wealthy man who sent her flowers and gifts and was madly in love with her. He begged her to go to bed with him, but she kept putting him off. Eventually she felt it was easier to give in and they fixed a date.

On the appointed night she dined with him, then they went to the theatre and ended up at her usual table in the Stork Club with a group. More and more people kept joining us and it was getting late. Her friend began to fidget with impatience.

"Tallulah," he pleaded, "you promised!"

"I know I did," she consoled him. "Tell you what. Everything is ready in my room at the hotel: champagne, soft lights, everything. Here is the key. You go up now and get into your pajamas. I have them all laid out for you. If I'm not there in an hour, start without me."

In 1968 Tallulah and I were in the ballroom of the Waldorf-Astoria among hundreds of theatrical people to meet the vice-presidential candidate Edmund Muskie. After a rather pompous introduction by his running mate, Hubert Humphrey, Muskie got up and slowly looked around at all the famous faces in the audience. "I feel like a mosquito in a nudist colony," he said at last. "I don't know where to start."

Tallulah was in terrible shape. I had to support her when we left but her spirit was bright. I escorted her home in a taxi and just before I left her she looked at me and said wistfully, "You know, daaaahling, we should have gotten together years ago. We should have married or at least lived together." She died not long after.

When we started work on *A Royal Scandal* she confessed that she was terrified of the camera. She told me that she could only be photographed from one side. I found she was right. One profile looked like Tallulah but the other like a completely different person.

The first cameraman on the picture was one of the best, Arthur Miller, a humorous little man who had once been a jockey. He had a solution. He put a light on his camera just above the lens.

"Miss Bankhead," he told her, "I have invented this light especially for you. In fact, we will call it the 'Bankhead'. It will make you look marvelous. You have nothing to worry about—just relax."

She was happy. She told everyone about the miraculous "Bankhead." When the picture was finished, Miller had the light crated. He gathered the crew together and they ceremoniously presented Tallulah with the "Bankhead" so she could use it in all her films.

Of course the light didn't, *couldn't* do anything. It amused Miller to contemplate how the cameraman on Tallulah's next film would handle the situation when she gave him the light. But she made only one more picture, twenty years later.

While we were filming *A Royal Scandal,* Anne Baxter asked if her grandfather could visit the set. He was the famous architect Frank Lloyd Wright. I agreed, but when he arrived Tallulah was upset.

She drew me aside. "Get that monster out of here," she told me fiercely. It was 1944, election year, and Tallulah was an ardent supporter of Roosevelt. "Wright is a right-wing reactionary Republican," she said, along with some unprintable adjectives. "I won't work while he is on the set."

"But Tallulah," I protested, "I can't throw him out." She was adamant. I suggested a compromise. Would she rehearse in front of him if I didn't shoot the scene? She agreed. I took a short scene between Tallulah and Anne Baxter and started to rehearse it. And rehearsed it and rehearsed it. Five times, ten times, twenty times, twenty-five times. Finally Frank Lloyd Wright got bored and left. Then I shot the scene.

Anne Baxter was about to get married to John Hodiak. They purchased a house. She invited a few people, among them her grandfather and me, to inspect it. After she had shown us around she asked her grandfather if he had any suggestions. "Yes," he said. "Burn it!"

*A Royal Scandal* was sneak-previewed in a little theatre some distance from Los Angeles. The audience laughed uproariously. Every joke worked. When it was over, however, I noticed that the people left the theatre quietly and subdued. I drove home with Lubitsch and Zanuck. They were delighted with the audience reaction. I was silent. Zanuck noticed it and asked me, "Why are you so quiet? We have a big hit."

"I don't think we have a big hit," was my answer.

"That's crazy! You heard how they laughed."

"They laughed," I agreed, "but they hated themselves for laughing."

I happened to be right. *A Royal Scandal* was not a great suc-

Otto, Linda Darnell, and Cornel Wilde, *Forever Amber*, 1947

Gypsy Rose Lee and her son Erik Preminger

Erik Preminger

Otto, Dana Andrews, Joan Crawford, and Henry Fonda (*Daisy Kenyon* © 1947 TWENTIETH CENTURY-FOX FILM CORPORATION. COURTESY OF TWENTIETH CENTURY-FOX)

Marilyn Monroe, Robert Mitchum, and Tommy Rettig (*River of No Return* © 1954 TWENTIETH CENTURY-FOX FILM CORPORATION. COURTESY OF TWENTIETH CENTURY-FOX)

Charles Coburn, William Eythe, and Tallulah Bankhead (*A Royal Scandal* © 1945 TWENTIETH CENTURY-FOX FILM CORPORATION. COURTESY OF TWENTIETH CENTURY-FOX)

Anne Baxter and Tallulah Bankhead (*A Royal Scandal* © 1945 TWENTIETH CENTURY-FOX FILM CORPORATION. COURTESY OF TWENTIETH CENTURY-FOX)

cess. The era of "the Lubitsch touch" was coming to an end. It was a change that Zanuck was not yet prepared to understand. Of course, Lubitsch was a first-rate film-maker, but in his films the humor was based on situations and not on character. The characters would do anything for a laugh, whether it was in keeping with what they represented or not. In *A Royal Scandal* the Empress of Russia behaved like no Empress of Russia ever would behave in order to produce laughs.

A big change had slowly taken place. Audiences wanted more than the chance to laugh. They wanted to see characters on the screen who behaved consistently.

The heart attack that Lubitsch suffered demoralized him, and he lived in terror of another one.

One night at a small dinner party in my house he got up after the first course and asked me to take him home at once.

"I'm dying," he said. "Please call my doctor." It turned out to be nothing but a mild indigestion.

Another friend, F. Hugh Herbert, the author of *The Moon Is Blue*, also had a heart attack but he reacted differently. He paid no attention to it and kept on living as usual. He even directed a play, which he had never attempted before. People asked him why he put such a strain on himself. "I don't care," he told them. "As long as I live I want to live without fear."

He lived for many more years and eventually died of cancer. Lubitsch, on the other hand, was killed by another heart attack less than three years after the first one.

# 15

## THE WOMEN OF HOLLYWOOD

Hollywood was hard on women. I don't speak of the ones usually considered as the casualties, those who were attracted to California from small towns all over America because they read that Lana Turner was discovered at a drugstore counter. They believed that they could become movie stars too, by just standing in the right place at the right moment. I am speaking of the women who did achieve the American dream, the ones who did become stars.

I have a reputation with women which is not entirely deserved, though it is true that I had my share of them, some of them stars. I never took out a woman while I was directing her in a play or a film, nor did I cast a girlfriend in any of my productions. I always kept my professional and my private lives separate.

Women stars in Hollywood were invariably in one of two categories. One group was made up of women who were exploited by men, and the other, much smaller group was composed of women who survived by acting like men.

I remember a small dinner party at a star's house. After dinner we watched a picture in her projection room. During the film I happened to look at her. She crooked a finger at me and left the room. I followed her into the bedroom and, without preamble, she seduced me, fixed her makeup, and led me back to the projection room. The important point was that neither of us made any pretense of love or had any obligation for continuing relations.

I remember another party in another star's house. I left early, explaining that I was starting a picture the next morning and had to get up very early. Around four in the morning my telephone rang. The hostess was on the line: "Everybody has left. Would you like to come over?" The distance between our houses was forty minutes by car. She summoned me that way several times while I was shooting. It gratified her that she could make me sacrifice my precious sleep for her. I didn't mind because she was very attractive.

A number of Hollywood's so-called sex symbols were not like their public image at all. Marilyn Monroe's off-camera personality was very different from what she represented on the screen. She was vulnerable and craved nothing more than affection.

Gene Tierney was born into wealth but her family lost everything in the 1929 crash when she was not quite ten years old. This experience stuck in her mind and resulted in extreme stinginess even after she had become a big star making several thousand dollars a week. One of the reasons her marriage to Oleg Cassini failed was because, instead of supporting his parents while he served in the Army, she got them jobs as extras, which didn't please the old Russian Count and Countess too much.

After her divorce, Gene fell in love with a young congressman, John F. Kennedy. He used to come to California to see her and she went East whenever she could to be with him. For about a year and a half they were devoted to one another and Gene was very happy.

We were starting the film *Whirlpool* in November 1949. She seemed very depressed. I asked her what the matter was. "It's all over," she told me. "His family won't let him marry me."

"Why?" I asked. "Because they are Catholic and you are divorced?"

"No. Because he is going to be President."

I laughed. "He's charming, he's bright, and he's rich but why should this young congressman become President of the United States?"

"Just watch," she said, very downcast. "If he isn't stopped by the back injury he suffered in the war, he'll be President."

Some years later I met Gene in Paris where she invited me to a house she had rented. It was obviously expensive, full of antique furnishings and staffed by expensive servants.

"What happened?" I teased her. "You're spending money?"

She told me confidentially and very happily: "In three months I'm going to marry Ali Khan." The affair ended suddenly. She had a nervous breakdown and spent a long time in the Menninger Clinic.

As part of her therapy she was advised to earn a living at a modest occupation. Her doctors thought it would help restore her self-confidence. She got a job in the Neiman-Marcus department store in Dallas, Texas. There she was seen by a wealthy man, Howard Lee, who had just been divorced from Hedy Lamarr. He married Gene. She improved so much in her mental outlook that she decided to try a film comeback. I offered her a part in *Advise and Consent*, which was filmed in Washington in 1961.

One day Pierre Salinger, Kennedy's press secretary, called and invited me and all members of the cast I wished to bring to have dinner with the President and Mrs. Kennedy on their yacht, the *Honey Fitz*. I accepted but remembered a short while later that we were to start night shooting on that date.

Very embarrassed, I asked if Mr. Salinger would explain the circumstances to the President and express my regrets. An hour later a message from the White House asked us to come the day after for lunch. I accepted.

Then my publicity man reminded me that I was scheduled to address a National Press Club luncheon on that day. I telephoned the president of the Press Club and asked him to postpone my speech.

"I cannot cancel the White House twice," I told him.

"We can't postpone your appearance. We have sold more tickets for your speech than for Khrushchev last month," he said. "But don't worry. Kennedy started his campaign at our Club. I'll fix it. Leave it to me." Salinger called shortly after and changed my luncheon date with the President for the day after my speech at the National Press Club.

*Time* magazine printed an article titled "The Arrogant Preminger," denouncing me for being so insolent that the President of the United States had to invite me three times before I would deign to accept. I didn't correct it, following my late father's advice to ignore malicious attacks. At the luncheon President Kennedy had my wife Hope on his right and Gene Tierney on his left. I sat across the table next to Mrs. Kennedy. The President and Gene were looking at each other most of the time, engrossed in a low-voiced conversation. They had not seen each other in all the years since their love affair ended.

As we were leaving, Gene's husband came up to me and said in his heavy Texas accent, "Mr. Preminger, I am really most grateful to you. As a Republican I never could have lunched at the White House without your help." I almost told him that his wife could easily arrange it at any time, but I refrained.

Another actress who suffered greatly after becoming a star was Maggie McNamara. She was a young fashion model when I cast her for the Chicago company of *The Moon Is Blue*. While she was performing in Chicago, the man she loved, a young radio writer, David Swift, commuted from New York every weekend during the eighteen months' run. She seemed a stable and happy person. Later I selected her to star in the film version. She signed a contract with Twentieth Century-Fox and after she made *The Moon Is Blue* she appeared in another successful film, *Three Coins in the Fountain*.

She had married Swift but when she started to make films something went wrong with their marriage. He left her for a French model they both had known in Chicago and Maggie was devastated. She had a nervous breakdown. When I saw her about seven years later she seemed changed. I gave her a small part in *The Cardinal* to help her get started again but it didn't work. She is now employed as a secretary for an insurance company.

Female stars lived in constant terror of growing older. In many cases wrinkles ended their career. Men had no such fears. John Wayne, Henry Fonda, Jimmy Stewart, and others in their late sixties are still stars. Hollywood actresses were always worried about being supplanted by younger women.

# 16

## MY SON ERIK

At the time I was making *Laura*, Gypsy Rose Lee was in Hollywood acting in a film, *Belle of the Yukon*. She was separated from her husband, Alexander Kirkland, and we went out together a few times. It wasn't a serious love affair, yet I was surprised to discover one day that she had returned to New York without saying goodbye to me.

On my next trip to New York I decided to call her and find out what had happened. Her maid answered the phone and told me Gypsy was in New York Hospital. When I reached her there she said: "This morning at six o'clock we had a son." It was the eleventh of December, 1944.

I was delighted. I immediately bought a big bunch of flowers and rushed to the hospital. I offered to support our son but she refused. "No, I don't want anything," she said. "I don't need anything. I can support my son myself. I want to bring him up to be my son only." Her statement was firm but without hostility.

Since her divorce from Alexander Kirkland was not yet final, the child's name was Erik Kirkland. She asked me to say nothing about my paternity but invited me to visit the boy whenever I was in New York. Three years later Gypsy married Julio de Diego, a Spanish painter. My visits to Erik became awkward and eventually stopped.

About ten years later I ran into Gypsy in London and took her to dinner. I asked her if she would not reconsider and tell Erik who his father really was.

Her answer was: "No, absolutely not. He thinks his father is Alexander Kirkland. Why disturb him?"

I had to accept her decision, but I asked her to put in her will that I was his father so that in case she died before me he would know whom to turn to. She agreed to that.

Toward the end of 1966 I worked on a screenplay based on John Hersey's novel *Too Far to Walk*. The book dealt with young people and LSD. I never made the film. My technical adviser on the script was a young man, Chuck Wein.

In the interest of research I even tried LSD myself. Timothy Leary gave it to me after a small dinner party in my home. While Hope was out of the room, Leary and two of his friends brought out some LSD pills and swallowed them. They offered me one.

Hope was shocked and frightened when she heard about it. Leary asked her to bring a candle, which he lit. He told me to look at the flame. He would be my guide, my guru, he explained. At that moment the candle slipped from his hand and fell on the rug. I was alarmed that he might set my house on fire under the influence of LSD. As tactfully as possible, I told him that I could not have a happy "trip" unless he and his friends left.

After Hope and I had gone to bed the LSD started to work. It was a strange sensation. I was aware that everything that happened was imaginary, but at the same time it seemed so clear and vivid that I could not doubt its reality. Hope seemed to shrink until she was the size of a small doll. I said to myself that she could not have become so tiny all of a sudden. But still there she was, only a few inches high.

A large drawing by Degas hangs on the wall opposite our bed. It shows the back of a nude woman, bent over washing her hair. Now I saw every bone in the woman's spine. I knew the spine was not there and still I saw it. It was like being faced with a double consciousness. When I woke up the next morning I asked Hope to call the office and cancel an appointment I had for ten o'clock. I didn't feel up to it.

"It's four o'clock in the afternoon," she said, still very worried.

"I canceled that appointment hours ago." It was evening before the LSD effects had completely gone.

One day in October 1966 I received a letter from my technical adviser Chuck Wein in which he told me that he had known a beautiful girl, Alexandra Kirkland, for some time. She had come to him to talk to him about a situation that had been troubling her and which concerned me. Her half brother Erik, whose mother was Miss Lee (Mr. Kirkland's wife at one time), had thought that his father was Kirkland until about a year and a half before, even though their relationship was strained. Evidently at some point Erik was told the true circumstances of his birth. He was pleased, but in retrospect obviously shocked—after all, at age eighteen or so it was quite a traumatic experience to learn that I was his father.

I learned later that Erik had asked Kirkland for money to buy a car and that Kirkland, rather than giving Erik the money, told Erik's psychoanalyst that he was not Erik's real father, that he would not provide Erik with any financial assistance either at that time or in the future, and that he would appreciate it if he would inform Erik of the true facts.

When Erik learned of the situation, he contacted Gypsy, who confirmed that Kirkland was not his father. Erik asked who his father was, but Gypsy refused to tell him. It was only after Erik persisted that Gypsy reluctantly told him, and even then, only after Erik promised to make no attempt to contact me.

After that, Erik drifted. He dropped out of college, lived in Greenwich Village, tried drugs and held minor jobs. Then he joined the Army.

As soon as I finished reading Wein's letter I called Gypsy. I pointed out that there was no reason any more for Erik and me not to meet. She gave me his address. He was stationed in Augsburg, Germany. I wrote him at once and asked if he would like to meet me. He replied promptly that he would be happy to meet me. We arranged a meeting in Paris during his next leave.

I was sixty years old and Erik was twenty-two. When he arrived at my hotel there was at first a strange, awkward feeling between us. But we were both so anxious to know and like one another that it soon evaporated. I noticed at once a marked physical resemblance. As we walked the streets of Paris and talked, an effortless understanding and rapport developed.

The next day Erik brought along his girlfriend, Barbara Ann Van Natten, a beautiful young stewardess. They married shortly afterward and had a son, Christopher, in 1968.

When he finished his time in the Army, Erik had a choice of either working on his mother's daytime TV show in San Francisco or taking a job with me. I was delighted when he chose me. He started to work as my casting director, my assistant, my story editor, and finally associate producer. He's charming, alert, intelligent, and a quick student.

Because of her television show, which had an audience made up largely of middle-aged housewives who might not approve, Gypsy asked us to keep Erik's story secret.

Before my reunion with Erik I had married for the third time, my first real marriage, and became the father of twins, Victoria and Mark. Explaining Erik's frequent visits to our house, I told them that he was my godson. To my great joy, they liked him and always welcomed him warmly. My wife Hope, who knew the truth, also felt affection for Erik and they got along well.

In 1970 Gypsy died of cancer. Now that she could no longer be hurt by the disclosure I wanted to adopt Erik. He agreed to it. My only worry was the reaction of the twins, who were then ten years old. How would they accept a sudden brother?

I told them one evening at dinner. Mark jumped up excitedly and dialed Erik's telephone number. When Erik answered he said: "Erik! Welcome to the family!" And Vicky beamed: "Wonderful. Now I'm an aunt."

Soon Erik, who is now Erik Preminger, wanted to branch out on his own. He was associate producer and played a part in a successful film, *The Heartbreak Kid*. Then he wrote the screenplay for my film *Rosebud*. After that he acquired the film rights to a book by John Gardner, *The Return of Moriarity,* and wrote the screenplay.

I consider finding Erik one of the best things that has happened to me in my life.

# 17

## LIFE IN THE SAUSAGE FACTORY

During my years in Hollywood toward the end of World War II each of the seven major studios was turning out between forty and fifty films a year. The demands of such volume required a certain practical adjustment to the realities of budget, shooting schedules, and available talent, all of which had to be attuned sensitively to the personality of the studio head.

As producers read manuscripts or books or plays, they considered—at least subconsciously—the likes and dislikes, the prejudices and quirks of the man who ran the studio. At Fox, for instance, all of us knew that Darryl Zanuck had no empathy for women in film. He liked women and was happily married but women's problems and feelings bored him totally.

At MGM producers avoided scripts containing sex or violence, both of which revolted Louis B. Mayer. He loved beautifully dressed women in his films, so they kept an eye out for stories about women wealthy enough to afford an expensive wardrobe.

Films are more varied today because the heads of the film companies don't put their personal imprint on the selection of scripts. They finance and distribute films.

Freedom of choice was in rather short supply at Twentieth Century-Fox under Darryl Zanuck. I was turning out a string of films following rules and obeying orders not unlike a foreman in a sausage factory. I went from picture to picture, usually taking with me a band of regulars on whom I had come to depend: cameraman Joe La Shelle, art director Lyle Wheeler, film editor Louis Loeffler, composer David Raksin, wardrobe designer Bonnie Cashin, and quite often Gene Tierney, Linda Darnell, and Dana Andrews.

*A Royal Scandal* was followed by *Fallen Angel,* which was followed by *Centennial Summer,* a Jerome Kern musical with a cast that included Linda Darnell, Jeanne Crain, Cornel Wilde, and Dorothy Gish, a great actress and delightful woman. Ernst Lubitsch died while he was directing *That Lady in Ermine* with Betty Grable and Douglas Fairbanks, Jr. I finished the film.

There was also *Daisy Kenyon.* I don't remember the story too well but it concerned, I think, a woman torn between two men. Joan Crawford had the title role and the men were Henry Fonda and Dana Andrews. Joan has a complex about heat. Her contract stipulated that the set had to be kept at an extremely low temperature. The two men were shivering and complained. The next day she bought them each a pair of long underwear.

She was very generous. When I came home after the first day of shooting I found my garden filled with beautiful new furniture. She had been to my house and noticed that the garden chairs were a little worn.

When the film was finished she gave me gold cuff links. I later discovered that she always gave her director cuff links at the conclusion of shooting. Once at a party there were four of us wearing identical sets.

I had a happy time making *Daisy Kenyon* with that remarkable, independent, and competent woman. The cast was a pleasure to direct, particularly Henry Fonda, who is completely professional.

I am also very fond of his daughter, Jane, who starred in *Hurry Sundown.* One time when we were on a TV talk show she said dreadful things about President Richard Nixon. I was not in favor of him either. However, I told her that no one should insult a President publicly. As it turned out much of what she said was understated.

My divorce from Marion made me eligible again and I became the target of several marriage proposals, one of which almost ended in tragedy. I had an affair with a beautiful young lady for more than a year. One night on our way home from a party she brought up the subject of marriage, as she had in the past. I repeated, as I had in the past, that I had no intention of marrying again. She opened the door and threatened to jump out of the car. We were traveling at better than sixty miles an hour. I could not stop because there were cars behind us. I managed to pull her back and close the door. I drove her home and told her that we had to stop seeing each other. A man who wanted to marry her, and eventually did, wrote a letter to Zanuck accusing me of beating the young woman. He threatened to knock me down the next time he saw me. Zanuck wanted to embarrass me and read the letter aloud in the executive dining room. Everybody laughed and so did I. A few nights later I went with another young lady to a restaurant for dinner. On our way to the dining area I saw my former girlfriend at the bar sitting next to the man who had sent the letter to Zanuck. I could not resist the temptation. "So you want to knock me down? Well, here I am," I said and slapped his face right and left. He was so surprised that he fell off the bar stool. It was a feast for the gossip columnists, who kept writing about it for weeks.

Subsequently I went steady for several months with a lovely young divorcée. She knew about my determination not to remarry. She called me one day while I was sitting in the dentist's chair. "Somebody is coming here in half an hour who wants to marry me." She named a famous writer. "If you still don't want me, I'll accept his proposal." "Do so," I advised her. They married soon afterward.

When a woman decides she is ready for marriage, nothing can stop her.

However, they didn't come to me only when they wanted to get married. A stunning young woman came to see me one day and explained calmly that she wanted to go to bed with me. As a child she used to listen night after night at the bedroom door when her mother and I were making love. She had made up her mind then to seduce me as soon as she was old enough. And she did.

# 18

## THE CENSORS

Hollywood films in those years right after World War II were full of puritan morality. Lovers kissed with their lips closed and were never seen in bed together even if married. There was a scene in my film *In the Meantime, Darling* which showed a husband and wife in a double bed, sleeping. I had a terrible fight to keep the scene in the film.

The hypocrisy extended to language, and to the moral code which demanded that anyone who misbehaved in the film had to be punished.

It was therefore daring of Fox to purchase the rights to the best-selling novel *Forever Amber* in 1946. It was an innocuous, trite story but the heroine had love affairs outside marriage and the book was condemned by the Roman Catholic Legion of Decency, the censorship office of the Catholic Church. It was risky to produce a film based on a banned book.

The film had been about six weeks in production at astronomical cost when I received a strangely urgent summons to spend the weekend with Zanuck at his house in Palm Springs.

I arrived Friday night. Zanuck waited until the next morning to tell me what he wanted. At breakfast there were three of us at the table: Zanuck, myself, and Charles Feldman, who was not only my agent but also the agent of John Stahl, who was directing *Forever Amber.*

"Stahl was doing a terrible job," Zanuck said in his usual blunt manner. "I have taken him off the picture." Feldman remained silent, offering no defense of his client. Zanuck continued, "I want you to take over. Please drive to the studio this afternoon. I have arranged for you to see all the film shot so far. Monday you will tell me what you want to do."

"I'll tell you now what I want to do," I said. "I want not to do *Forever Amber.* I read the book when it was sent around by the story department. I found it terrible."

Zanuck glared at me. He pointed out that I was one of the highest-paid producer-directors at the studio, with a unique no-option contract that still had six years to run. I was guaranteed handsome raises every year. "You're a member of the team," he told me sternly. "You must do it. I won't blame you if it doesn't turn out well." I had no choice.

When I saw what had been shot I felt even worse about the picture. Zanuck had discovered a young English actress for the lead. She was amateurish beyond belief. The script was equally appalling.

I met Zanuck in his office Monday morning. "First of all," I told him, "I must have a new script. That will mean a delay of two to three months. And the woman who plays Amber—"

"You're right," Zanuck interrupted me. "We'll throw her out. Let's think about her replacement while you go ahead with the new script."

I later discovered that he had already decided that it would be Linda Darnell but did not mention it at this point in case I disagreed.

William Perlberg was the producer but he kept out of my way. I pulled a writer, Philip Dunne, off the script he was working on and in addition hired Ring Lardner, Jr. Between the three of us we put together a fairly good script.

Meanwhile, Zanuck broke it to me that Linda Darnell would play the lead. I didn't think she was right for the part. I protested vigorously. My choice was Lana Turner, who was under contract to MGM but probably could be borrowed.

Zanuck refused. Whoever played the part of Amber would immediately become a superstar, he said. He would not give such an opportunity to an actress not under contract to him.

I didn't give up. I gave a dinner party and I invited Zanuck and Lana Turner, who very much wanted the role. "It's up to you now," I advised her. She did her best. She flirted shamelessly with Zanuck, at one point even sitting on his lap. But he would not change his mind.

I had Linda Darnell's hair dyed blond and started the film. It went on and on, the longest shooting schedule I ever had. Zanuck was determined that this would be the biggest and most expensive and most successful film in history.

One redeeming factor was that I met Leon Shamroy on that picture, a brilliant cameraman and a marvelous friend. We later made many films together.

Because the book was objectionable from the Catholic point of view, we were very careful to stay well within the rules of the industry's own censoring body, The Motion Picture Producers and Distributors of America Code Administration, then commonly known as the Hays Office after its first president, Will H. Hays. The result was so inoffensive that the film easily secured its approval.

The Catholic Legion of Decency, however, condemned it. The Legion no longer exists, at least not in that form, but at the time it decided not only what books Catholics should not read but also what films they should not see.

Spyros Skouras, the president of Twentieth Century-Fox asked me to come to New York for the critical meeting with the Legion of Decency. There were three priests in his office when I arrived, one of them a handsome man of about thirty-five who was the head of the Legion.

Skouras pleaded with him. Fox had spent six million dollars on the picture, he said. It would be a crushing financial blow to the studio if the Legion did not relent.

The priest was cool. The book had been banned, he said, so Fox should have known better than to make the movie.

Skouras was so frantic that he came around his desk and knelt in front of the priest. He kissed his hand. "Father, Father," he begged, "please help!"

The priest considered for a moment. Then he said, "All right. Maybe we can accept the film if you change the title."

Skouras groaned. "If we change the title we have nothing!" he protested. "We must keep the title!" He had some yellow worry beads in one hand and kept twisting them through his fingers. Then he actually began to cry.

"Please go into the projection room with Mr. Preminger. He will make any change you want. Just show him what you want cut and he'll cut it."

It was painful. We stopped after each reel while the priest listed his objections. He wanted all the love scenes cut at the point where the couple was about to kiss. He would not allow the lips to touch. He also required an introduction to the film to be shot which he wrote. It stated that everything that happened was imaginary, or some such nonsense.

We maintained a friendly mood throughout the session, which took all day. Skouras' behavior had embarrassed him as much as it had me.

With the Legion of Decency's approval *Forever Amber* opened in over nine hundred theatres all over America on the same day. In its first week it grossed over six million dollars, to the enormous relief of Twentieth Century-Fox.

That pathetic scene in Skouras' office was very much on my mind when I made my first picture as an independent, *The Moon Is Blue,* and had to confront the Legion of Decency's veto again.

The year 1951 was a turning point in the history of films in America. The dictatorial power of the studio heads was broken by the famous "consent decree." It followed the government's antitrust suit against the major companies, charging them with a monopoly. They had to separate the ownership of theatres from production and distribution of films. They had to give up one or the other. Theatres became autonomous and started to bid for films competitively. Independent producers could at last make pictures and have them exhibited.

I was one of the first to take advantage of the opportunity. I went to my agent Charles Feldman and asked him to negotiate with Zanuck the release from my contract for six months of every year so that I could make pictures independently.

Feldman didn't like it. "If that's what you want, you go to Zanuck yourself," he told me. "I'm not going to help you ruin your career. You have the best contract my agency has ever secured for a director. If you want to throw it out the window, do it yourself."

So I did. Zanuck agreed to put me on half salary and half time for the five years remaining on my contract. Feldman commented sourly, "You'll wind up directing plays on Broadway again." His hundred per cent Hollywood mind couldn't think of anything lower.

*The Moon Is Blue*, F. Hugh Herbert's enchanting romantic comedy, opened in 1951 in the Henry Miller Theatre on Broadway and ran for 924 performances.

Herbert gave me the play in Hollywood. I contacted Richard Aldrich and Richard Myers, who agreed to produce it with me. I was not satisfied with the third act and made Herbert promise me to rewrite it no matter what the reviews said or how well the audiences liked it out of town.

Sometimes a play has a major fault which is easy to fix, and other times there are little things, such as inconsistencies in the characters, which require major rewrites. I have never known a script which was so perfect that it could be put on the stage as it was originally written. In the case of *The Moon Is Blue*, I thought the third act would have to be redone from scratch.

We opened in Wilmington, Delaware. The audience loved the play and the reviews were sensational. My mind was unchanged and Herbert kept his word. When we moved the play to Boston, our next stop before the New York opening, he locked himself in his hotel room. In a week he turned out a completely new third act. All the time he was writing and we were rehearsing it, Boston audiences cheered the old one. Herbert, however, had faith in my judgment. With the new third act we brought the play to Broadway and triumph.

*The Moon Is Blue* was my choice for my first independent film. I secured the backing of United Artists, which had just been reorganized under the leadership of Arthur Krim and Robert Benjamin, two partners of the Louis Nizer law firm. They had very little money to invest so the film was budgeted at only $240,000.

To save costs, William Holden agreed to do it without a salary and gambled instead on a large percentage of the profits. David Niven was paid very little, plus a small percentage. Holden was big box office at that time but Niven's last film was a failure.

Arthur Krim was so alarmed when he heard that I had signed Niven that he flew to California and begged me to allow him to pay Niven off with United Artists' money, at no cost to my budget.

I told him not to worry. Niven would be a big success in the part. He had played the role on stage in the San Francisco company and gave, in my opinion, the best performance of all the actors who played Donald Slater in the eight companies that toured *The Moon Is Blue* in the United States and Canada.

Of all the actresses I chose Maggie McNamara of the Chicago company. I thought she would bring to the screen the innocent, virginal look that was needed. I was afraid that Barbara Bel Geddes, who acted the role to perfection on Broadway, would not look young enough on camera.

I made an unprecedented contract with United Artists for *The Moon Is Blue.* I demanded and received complete autonomy and the right to the final cut of the film. Nobody could overrule my decisions. I had at last the freedom I had always wished for.

Scripts had to be submitted to the Hays Office before shooting started. The script of *The Moon Is Blue* was rejected. Unless I changed six lines the Hays Office would withhold its Seal of Approval.

Zanuck heard about it and tried to be helpful. "I'll do it for you," he offered. "After all, it is only six lines."

"Not one line, not one frame," I told him flatly, remembering how Skouras had caved in so pathetically. "I have the right of free expression," I told him. "I will not accept any censorship, private or official. It should really be called precensorship, telling the producer in advance what he can and what he cannot put into a film. It's against the Constitution. If my picture is obscene, we have laws to cover the situation. I can be arrested, the picture confiscated, and a court convict me if I'm found guilty."

The Catholic Legion of Decency, with which the Hays Office always cooperated closely, added its disapproval of the script.

Looking back, it is laughable what all those people found objectionable: the frequent mention of the word "virgin," for instance, the word "seduce," and the word "pregnant."

Zanuck warned me, "You're being silly. Without the Seal there won't be five theatres in the United States that will show your film."

*The Moon Is Blue* had played on Broadway and in theatres all over the country. American audiences found it amusing and were not shocked. I did not believe that movie audiences were different or that they should be protected from something freely available on the stage. The language in the film was exactly the same as the language in the play.

I didn't negotiate with the Catholic Legion of Decency. If they wanted to instruct Catholics not to see the film, fine. They had every right to do so. But I am not Catholic and they could not tell me what to take out of my pictures.

United Artists behaved very well. Though they were nervous, they supported me. They defied the industry's censor and declared they would distribute *The Moon Is Blue* without the Seal.

We went ahead. To save costs I first rehearsed the cast for three weeks and was able to shoot the film in twenty-four days. I did a German version simultaneously with Johanna Matz and Hardy Krüger, who afterward became important film and stage stars in their country.

My old friend Gregory Ratoff played a small part, a taxi driver, in both versions. Since he spoke German with a Russian accent, I later dubbed in my own voice for his. The German version was called *Die Jungfrau auf dem Dach,* which means "The Virgin on the Roof."

The furor over *The Moon Is Blue* was intense even before its release. I spent much of my time defending it on radio and television. I explained over and over that it wasn't in the least obscene or lewd. It was a lighthearted, harmless comedy.

However, when I saw the advertising campaign United Artists had prepared I was outraged. They showed in most of the ads a half-nude girl, strongly suggesting that the movie after all was pornographic. At that time I met Saul Bass, a graphic designer who had just moved from New York to the West Coast. He designed another campaign. The central idea was a window with the blind down and two little birds perched on the sill, peeking behind the blind.

He has since done the logo and campaign for almost all my films and plays. He is the best graphic artist I know.

Like Moss Hart, he is a gentle, warm man of great charm and intelligence. He has one vice only, he is always late. At one time I was in London and asked him to bring me the campaign for *The Cardinal* by a certain date. He sent me a cable as he left Los Angeles announcing his arrival in London the day I had set. I was surprised and proud of him.

The next day he telephoned me from New York. Just as he was boarding the transatlantic plane there for the second leg of his journey he discovered that he had brought his wife's passport instead of his own. He had to wait twenty-four hours for his passport. Fate is against Saul Bass being on time ever.

When *The Moon Is Blue* was released it was denounced from pulpits of Catholic churches as evil. In small towns priests stood outside the theatres taking down the names of parishioners who went in. As a result the box office suffered somewhat in small communities, but in cities *The Moon Is Blue* was a huge success.

A few years ago CBS wanted to buy *The Moon Is Blue* for television. They then changed their minds because the picture was still condemned by the Church, though they didn't admit that was their reason. I would not approach the Church to change the rating, under any circumstances, but the lawyer for the estate of F. Hugh Herbert arranged to have the rating changed. It then played on the network twice, without any cuts.

*The Man with the Golden Arm* was my second fight against the absurd censorship that Hollywood still tried to impose.

When I read the novel by Nelson Algren about a heroin addict I decided to make the film, although I was aware that the Hays Office code expressly outlawed even the mere mention of drugs on the screen. Because of this restriction the actor John Garfield, who had acquired the rights, never made the picture. I bought them from his estate.

Nelson Algren came to Hollywood to work on the script with me. I arranged for him to stay in a comfortable hotel near the Columbia Studio where I had my office at the time. He moved in, but when I telephoned him the next day I was told that he

had checked out. After a while he called me. He had moved
downtown to a disreputable, broken-down, flea-ridden hotel full
of pimps, addicts, and drunks.

"Why?" I asked him, amazed.

"I couldn't stay in that fancy place," he explained. "This suits
me better."

He was an amusing, intelligent man but he couldn't write dialogue or visualize scenes. He was purely a novelist, a storyteller.
I had to get another writer, Walter Newman, to prepare the
script.

Algren was furious when he saw the result. He felt I had done
violence to his book, as Vera Caspary did when she read the
script of *Laura*. When a producer buys the rights to a book or a
play he owns it. The property rights are transferred, as in any
sale. The writer gives up his control, as the word "sell" implies.

When I prepare a story for filming it is being filtered through
my brain, my emotions, my talent such as I have. Some characters don't interest me so I drop them, others who are minor in
the book appeal strongly to me and I develop them to become
more active. I may create new characters altogether. I have no
obligation, nor do I try, to be "faithful" to the book.

When we had about seventy pages of script for *The Man with
the Golden Arm*, I sent copies to the agents of the two actors I
thought most suitable for the lead, Marlon Brando and Frank
Sinatra. I asked them, if they were interested, to keep their time
free, pending completion of the script.

Two days later Sinatra's agent called me. Sinatra wanted to do
the picture, he said. "Fine," I told him. "As soon as the script is
finished I'll send it to you."

"You don't understand," the agent explained. "Sinatra is ready
to sign the contract right now. He doesn't need to see the rest of
the script."

We made the deal and I announced the news that Sinatra
would play the part, whereupon Brando's agent telephoned me.
He was upset. "Why didn't you wait?" he said. "I haven't even
had time to give the script to Brando."

I wanted Kim Novak for the female lead. She had done two
successful pictures for Columbia, where she was under contract.
She had very little confidence in her ability to act and her assur-

ance was not improved by the directors of her first pictures. They paid little attention to the way she delivered her lines on the stage and dubbed them later, having her repeat them over and over until they thought they were acceptable. I don't believe in that method.

I thought she was right for the part so I went to Harry Cohn, chief of Columbia and one of Hollywood's slave masters.

Harry Cohn and I had a love-hate relationship. He was a profane man. In order to disarm him I always recited his favorite four-letter words the minute I saw him. He gave me an office at his studio, but I never made a picture for him. Sometimes I drove him home after work, trailed by his chauffeured limousine, and from time to time he asked my advice.

One evening he told me he had acquired the rights to William Inge's Broadway hit *Picnic*. He wanted my opinion of the director he planned to sign.

"How can you!" I protested. "Josh Logan did a beautiful job in New York and he is the only one who should direct the film."

Cohn made some remarks about Logan's health and the fact that he had never directed a film. I brushed them aside. "Try Logan," I urged him. "If it doesn't work out I'll do the film for free."

He hired Logan, who made a great success of *Picnic* and established himself as film director.

Cohn was reluctant to let me have Kim Novak for *The Man with the Golden Arm*. We argued for a while and then he said I could have her for $100,000, at that time a staggering amount for a young actress. I agreed to it.

When I notified Sinatra that we were starting rehearsals of the film he said, "Ludvig"—which is what he always calls me, mispronouncing my middle name—"I am not an actor, I can't rehearse. I try to do it the best I can and that's it."

"Anatole," I told him, using the name I inexplicably call him, "come at ten tomorrow morning and I will teach you how to rehearse."

He was surprised to discover that he loved rehearsals. He could not get enough. When I wanted to quit he would ask, "Let's do it again, just once, please!"

There was only one time when Sinatra balked. We had just

Harry Belafonte, Dorothy Dandridge, and Pearl Bailey (*Carmen Jones* © 1954 CARLYLE PRODUCTIONS. COURTESY OF TWENTIETH CEN-TURY-FOX)

Sidney Poitier, Sammy Davis, Jr., Dorothy Dandridge, Brock Peters, Pearl Bailey, Diahann Carroll (holding baby), *Porgy and Bess*, 1959 (SAMUEL GOLDWYN PRODUCTIONS)

Jean Seberg, *Saint Joan*, 1957 (copyright © 1957, UNITED ARTISTS CORPORATION)

James Stewart, Joseph N. Welch, Lee Remick, and George C. Scott, *Anatomy of a Murder*, 1959 (CARLYLE PRODUCTIONS. PHOTO BY MILL)

The Duke and Duchess of Windsor, Otto, and Joseph N. Welch on the set of *Anatomy of a Murder*, 1959 ( COLUMBIA PICTURES )

finished a very difficult long scene to my satisfaction. The head electrician approached me and told me that one of his men had made a mistake. We would have to do it again. When I told Sinatra he blew his top and said he wouldn't. He had done it right, I had okayed it, and as far as he was concerned that was it.

I followed him as he stormed into his dressing room. "Look, Anatole, what do you want me to do? Kill the electrician? He's entitled to make a mistake, the same as you or I."

He came out with me and apologized to the electrician and we did the scene again.

He was compassionate about Kim Novak's extreme nervousness in front of the camera. She was terrified, and though she tried very hard she had great difficulty delivering her lines believably. Sometimes we had to do even very short scenes as often as thirty-five times. Throughout the ordeal Sinatra never complained and never made her feel that he was losing patience.

Many years later Paramount asked me to direct *The Godfather*. I thought Sinatra would be wonderful in the lead and sent him the book. I even offered to eliminate the character of the singer, who some people thought was patterned after Sinatra. Nevertheless he said, "Ludvig, I pass on this."

I didn't want to do it without him so I passed too. It was a reversal of *The Man with the Golden Arm* case. This time Brando got the plum role and Sinatra lost out.

Sinatra is an extraordinary man. I am fond of him although our relationship faded in recent years because of a misunderstanding between us that his agent-lawyer created.

The Hays Office made no secret of its opposition to *The Man with the Golden Arm*. It was clear from the first day of shooting that the Seal of Approval would be withheld. The Hays people naturally expected the support of the Catholic Legion of Decency, but the Legion approved the picture. The Legion most likely wanted to avoid losing another battle after *The Moon Is Blue*.

*The Man with the Golden Arm* was released without the Seal but had no difficulty finding theatres all over America. It became one of the biggest successes United Artists ever had.

The issue of censorship was tested in the courts. There were two cases, Kansas vs. *The Moon Is Blue* and Maryland vs. *The Man with the Golden Arm.* Both went to the Supreme Court and established freedom of expression for motion pictures.

# 19

## BLACKLIST

My stand against censorship was founded on two principles. One was my autonomy as producer and director. In Vienna I had enjoyed complete creative control of my productions and my frustrations under a Hollywood studio contract were painful. I was reduced almost to a puppet. I was not able to cast without interference. When the picture was finished I was denied final cut, which meant I was helpless to protect my work. I had to accept and even collaborate when Spyros Skouras asked the priest-censor to do as he pleased with *Forever Amber* after I had spent ten months working on the film. But there was something far more important at stake than my personal freedom in a creative medium.

Freedom of expression is the most powerful defense of democracy. No totalitarian government, right or left, can exist without censorship. It must firmly control the speech and writing of its citizens. When Senator Joseph McCarthy was playing on the uncertainty of Cold War fears by charging that America was riddled with Communist spies, the consequence was a repression of dissent and a black period in the history of American liberty. The studio heads in Hollywood were among the first to panic.

It began in the spring of 1947 when the chairman of the House Un-American Activities Committee, J. Parnell Thomas, came to California to look for Communists. It was an old hunting ground for him. He believed the entertainment industry to be a breeding ground for sedition. He had once attacked the Federal Theater as a hotbed of "Communism and the New Deal."

He talked to people about the Screen Writers' Guild, which indeed had a number of members who attended Communist cell meetings. Membership in the Communist Party was legal, but most of those who attended the meetings or joined the Party were actually liberals who thought that some aspects of Communism would relieve social injustice. They had no intention to overthrow the government.

Congressman Thomas returned to Washington with some names and his committee began to subpoena writers to testify if they were, or ever had been, members of the Communist Party. If they refused to answer they could be charged with contempt; if they answered in the negative some of them exposed themselves to charges of perjury; if they answered in the affirmative they were required to name others.

Ring Lardner, Jr., was one of the first to be summoned. Lardner was a gifted screenwriter who won an Academy Award in 1942 for the Katharine Hepburn-Spencer Tracy film *Woman of the Year*. He interrupted work with me on the script of *Forever Amber* to go to Washington. His testimony before the congressional committee is full of interruptions. He refused to discuss whether or not he had been a member of the Communist Party. As a descendant of one of the Minutemen at Lexington he didn't see how he could be labeled un-American. What he tried in vain to read into the record was a statement that the committee was behaving in an un-American way by attacking the freedom of American citizens.

Studio heads, alarmed at the possibilities of guilt by association, met secretly at the Waldorf-Astoria in New York and drew up a list of screenwriters, directors, producers, and performers that they believed to have Communist sympathies. It was agreed that everyone on the list would be fired and blacklisted.

Lardner and I were working in my office at Fox about a week later. My secretary, Mary Cook, interrupted to say that Zanuck wanted to see Lardner at once.

I was surprised that the request didn't include me. I asked her to check if there was some mistake. She returned to say there wasn't. "Mr. Zanuck wants to see Mr. Lardner alone."

Lardner was back in five minutes. "I have just been fired," he said.

It was the beginning of dismissals all over Hollywood. The original blacklist was growing; eventually it contained more than four hundred names. There was so much fear in the industry that it was considered dangerous not only to hire a suspected Communist but even to communicate with one.

The morning after I had dined with Lardner in a Los Angeles restaurant my telephone rang repeatedly with calls from friends urging me in my best interest not to be seen with him again in public. "My conscience is clear," I told them. And I continued to go out with him.

There is no doubt that the Screen Writers' Guild was infested with radicals. The most extreme formed a clique that promoted writers who agreed with their views and excluded those who didn't. An agent, who later was indicted for contempt of Congress because he refused to reveal whether he was a member of the Communist Party, once pressed upon me a writer who was not even his client. He turned out to be totally incompetent. During ten weeks in my employ he didn't write a single line. Later he told the congressional committee that he had been a member of the Communist Party. He was one of the first to name others and betray many of his former friends for the price of immunity.

Ring Lardner, Jr., and nine others were the "Hollywood Ten" who went to prison for contempt. Ironically, Lardner met there Congressman Parnell Thomas, convicted for graft. The "Hollywood Ten" found after their release that their punishment had only begun. They and hundreds of others could find no work anywhere. By using pseudonyms, writers could continue to feed their families, but performers were destroyed. Gale Sondergaard, wife of one of the "Hollywood Ten," disappeared from the screen. So did Howard Da Silva.

When I learned how many people of liberal views had been invited to Communist cell meetings, I asked Ring Lardner why I had never been asked.

He grinned. "We knew you wouldn't play."

"How did you know?" I persisted.

"Well," he said, "we just knew."

They sized up the people they tried to recruit. They knew that no matter how liberal my views were I would never get involved with Communism.

The existence of the blacklist embarrassed the studio heads and they persistently denied it, even pretending that they never met at the Waldorf-Astoria to draw it up. I got proof to the contrary when I made a deal with Fox for the distribution of my independent film, *Carmen Jones.* The contract, as usual, gave me complete autonomy, but Fox insisted on one condition: I had to submit the names of everyone I intended to hire, *everyone,* to their legal department, which would have the right to veto without giving any reason. It wasn't a question of artistic choice. It was the secret blacklist. If your name was on it, you didn't work.

For years after it was discredited, McCarthyism remained a blight on the industry. In 1959 I hired Dalton Trumbo to write the screenplay for *Exodus.* One of the "Hollywood Ten," he was making a meager living by working at low fees under assumed names. He and Michael Wilson, who collaborated on several scripts in their exile, received between $1,000 and $1,500 for an entire screenplay. Under the pseudonym "Robert Rich," Trumbo won an Academy Award in 1957 for *The Brave One.* When the award was announced, no one came forward to claim it. The Academy finally sent him the Oscar eighteen years later, in 1975.

United Artists financed and distributed *Exodus.* I made a luncheon date with its president and chairman, Arthur Krim and Robert Benjamin. I told them: "Trumbo has done a first-rate job on this script. You people are always saying that the blacklist is fiction, so I will give him the credit he deserves. I shall use his real name as the sole author of the script."

They behaved very well. Krim said, "You have the right to do this. We can't support you but we are not going to stop you."

When the film was released, Trumbo's name on the credits caused a sensation. There were pickets outside the theatre in Boston and elsewhere, but the picture didn't suffer. It was Trumbo's first screen credit in fifteen years. I reasoned that he had paid his debt to society when he served his prison term.

Now he had the right again to make a living in his chosen profession like any other citizen.

The next picture he wrote was *Spartacus*. There was no difficulty about using his real name and from then on he was able to demand proper payment for his screenplays.

With Trumbo's emergence, other banned writers and performers began to surface again. But their numbers were few. Some had committed suicide, some had become alcoholics, and many had lost their self-confidence.

The reason I fought censorship was not because I thought that a few cuts or changes in a film would destroy an artistic masterpiece, but because I believe that permitting those cuts would be a step, no matter how small, toward the loss of our liberty.

# 20

## THE THIRTEENTH LETTER AND
## A FORGETTABLE MARRIAGE

In 1950 I made a film in Quebec, *The Thirteenth Letter*. It was based on a story by Louis Chavance and a film by Henri-Georges Clouzot, *Le Corbeau*. It was the first time that a Hollywood picture was shot in its entirety on location.

We had an outstanding cast. I still remember how much I enjoyed working with Charles Boyer and Françoise Rosay. One of the leads was played by a British actor, Michael Rennie. During the filming he was visited several times by a pretty New York model, Mary Gardner. Gradually her attention switched from him to me.

I married Mary Gardner on the fourth of December, 1951. We were divorced in 1958. A forgettable marriage.

# 21

## HOWARD HUGHES WAS
## NOT THAT ECCENTRIC

I had just finished *The Thirteenth Letter* and was reading stories
for my next Fox assignment when Zanuck summoned me to his
office. He told me that Howard Hughes, who owned the RKO
Studio at the time, wanted me to make a film for him. Zanuck
had already agreed to lend him my services. He handed me a
script entitled "Murder Story." I read it and found it very bad.
The next day I returned to Zanuck and told him that I would
have no part of it. Zanuck pleaded with me. He was indebted to
Hughes for many favors financially and otherwise and wanted to
show his gratitude by making him a friendly gift of me. But I
remained firm.

That night, about three in the morning, my telephone rang:
Hughes wanted to see me. He picked me up half an hour later in
a battered old Chevrolet so noisy that you had to speak very
loud to be heard. That suited Hughes, who was hard of hearing
but didn't want to admit it.

He drove me around the deserted streets for hours. He explained that he wanted a well-known actress, who was under
contract to him, to play the lead. However, her contract was to
expire within three months. During those three months she was
committed to only eighteen shooting days. As we kept on driving
he confessed that he had had a violent quarrel with her. In a fit

of anger she had grabbed a pair of scissors and cut her hair to the roots, being well aware that he despised short hair on women.

Now he wanted to squeeze one more film out of her before she left RKO. "I'm going to get even with that little bitch," he said, "and you must help me. I went to Darryl for advice and he recommended you. He said you are the only director I could rely on to complete her role in eighteen shooting days. Look, you walk in to the studio tomorrow morning like Hitler. It's yours. You hire any writer you want to, any number of writers to rewrite the script, as long as they are not Commies. Nobody will interfere with you and that includes me. All I want to see is a test of the lady wearing a wig of long beautiful black hair." I finally accepted. He was a persuasive man.

I changed the title to *Angel Face*. Frank Nugent and Oscar Millard worked with me on the new script. The actress was most cooperative. I enjoyed working with her.

I wanted Harry Stradling to be the cameraman on the picture. He was fast, and particularly good at photographing women. He was under contract to Goldwyn, who was willing to lend him to us. But Stradling balked. He had just finished a picture and was tired. He needed a rest and financially it did not mean anything because under his contract with Goldwyn he was paid by the week regardless of whether he worked or not.

"What would you like?" I asked him. He thought for a moment, then he said, "For a long time I have been planning a trip to Europe with my wife. If you can get us two tickets on TWA from Hughes I will do the film with enthusiasm." Hughes owned TWA at the time. I tried to telephone Hughes all through the day and the following night. In vain. So I took the chance and promised Stradling the tickets. If Hughes said no I could buy them and charge them to the budget as part of Stradling's pay. However, when I finally reached Hughes there was no problem. "Give him the airline," he told me.

When Stradling and his wife, after finishing the picture, went to the Los Angeles airport to leave on their vacation they were welcomed by a TWA vice-president with flowers. In Paris another TWA executive waited for them with a limousine and took them to a hotel suite. When they left the hotel their bill had been paid. The same routine repeated itself on each stop until they returned home.

Hughes was very generous as long as he did not suspect that people were trying to exploit him. If he thought that somebody—partner or employee—was trying to take advantage of him he reacted without mercy. Many people like to make money because they enjoy spending it and living well. But the very rich—the real moneyman—uses money as a weapon; he worships it as a symbol of his superiority and power. He believes it elevates him to a special status high above the ordinary mortal.

Though Hughes owned RKO, he never appeared there. He rented an office at the Goldwyn Studio, with a projection room of his own. He spent many nights there making telephone calls and watching films. He never used a projectionist. He operated the equipment himself, commuting between the projection booth and the theatre.

Howard Hughes was extremely successful with women, partly because of his quiet charm, partly because of his money, and mostly because of his persistence. One day he called Linda Darnell's agent, Bill Schiffrin, and told him he wanted to meet her. Schiffrin was impressed. "But of course, Mr. Hughes." Linda Darnell, however, refused. "I know what he wants," she told her agent. "But I am married. My contract with Twentieth Century-Fox has several years to run, so I don't need to know him." Hughes found out that she took golf lessons. He was one of the best golfers around. Nevertheless, he enrolled in the same course. When she saw him there she naturally felt flattered. He introduced himself. "Why are you so difficult?" he asked. "What harm could there be in the two of us having lunch together?" "All right," she told him, "if my agent can come along." They made a date for Hughes to call for her the next day at noon. He arrived promptly in his old Chevrolet and drove her and Schiffrin to his airfield. Waiting for them with the engines warming up was a Constellation, one of the largest planes then in use. "What's going on?" asked an alarmed Linda Darnell. "We are going to lunch," Hughes answered, as though going to lunch in a Constellation was perfectly normal. They boarded the plane: no pilot, no co-pilot, no one but the three of them. Hughes took the controls and flew the plane to San Francisco. There was a car waiting for them. They were driven to the Fairmont Hotel, which has a spectacular view of the city and the bay. Hughes had taken an entire floor of the hotel. A small orchestra played, a delicious buffet was laid out, and waiters served them with great solicitude.

I don't know exactly what happened except that Linda got a divorce from her cameraman husband a few months later.

Marriage was one human condition Hughes wanted to avoid at any price. Once he was at a cocktail party in my house and asked me to introduce him to a beautiful young actress who had just arrived in town. He had a number of phrases for such occasions and tried one on her. "Miss Marshall," he said at his charming best, "from now on you are going out only with me." "Yes, Mr. Hughes," she replied without hesitation, "so long as you are going out only with me." He was so terrified that he turned around and left the party.

When we finished shooting *Angel Face* I made a rough cut and then had to go to San Francisco for a few days. When I returned I found a note from Hughes on my desk. "Saw your rough cut. It's brilliant. Howard." I hit the ceiling. Hughes had no right to see the rough cut. I called the editor. He explained to me what happened. At RKO the editors were instructed to leave a note on their desk every evening when they left describing in detail the progress they had made so far on the film they were working on. Hughes had a driver with a passkey to all the cutting rooms. He would check and report to Hughes, who would instruct him, if he wanted to see one of those unfinished prints, to bring it to his projection room at the Goldwyn Studio.

It was unethical. It violated the Screen Directors' Guild of America contract in particular, but all in all Howard Hughes was a fascinating man and I am glad to have known him.

# 22

## MARILYN MONROE

*River of No Return* was a picture that I owed Darryl Zanuck under the terms of my revised contract. After the complete freedom I had enjoyed making *The Moon Is Blue* as an independent and the almost-freedom Howard Hughes had given me in order to take revenge on an actress I found myself more reluctant than I had expected to be back at Fox.

The cast was a consolation, Robert Mitchum and Marilyn Monroe, and, better still, the film was to be shot almost entirely on location in Canada.

In the summer of 1953 I arrived with cast and crew on a special train in Banff, a small town in the Alberta Rockies. A large crowd of excited Canadians gathered from miles around to greet us.

Marilyn Monroe had just finished a run of pictures, *Niagara, Gentlemen Prefer Blondes,* and *How to Marry a Millionaire,* which made her one of the biggest stars in Hollywood. She was traveling with an entourage consisting of Joe DiMaggio, who was in love with her, a friend of DiMaggio's who was a Broadway ticket broker and was along to keep the baseball hero company during the long hours when Marilyn was working, and Marilyn's drama coach, a woman named Natasha Lytess.

I first encountered Natasha Lytess in the dining car of the special train that brought us from California. She was passing herself off as a Russian, for reasons of her own, but she was in fact German.

Marilyn's ambition was to become a great dramatic actress. She underrated her natural magic in front of the camera. As a result, she always employed a coach. One of them was Paula Strasberg, who, with her husband, started the New York Actors Studio that promoted the "method" style of acting. Marilyn clung to these coaches and accepted blindly any advice they gave her, most of which was bad.

Natasha had a theory that Marilyn should not speak in the soft, slurred voice that was so much part of the unique image she projected on the screen. She wanted her to enunciate every syllable distinctly. Marilyn didn't question Natasha's judgment. She rehearsed her lines with such grave ar-tic-yew-lay-shun that her violent lip movements made it impossible to photograph her. Natasha applauded her on her marvelous pronunciation, which inspired Marilyn to exaggerate even more.

I pleaded with her to relax and speak naturally but she paid no attention. She listened only to Natasha. I began to detest Natasha with a passion but there was nothing I could do. Monroe was the top box office attraction. If she wanted Natasha on the set, Fox gave her Natasha on the set.

Robert Mitchum saved the situation. During rehearsals he ignored her studied affectation. Then, just as I was ready to shoot, he would slap her sharply on the bottom and snap, "Now stop that nonsense! Let's play it like human beings. Come on!" He managed to startle her and she dropped, at least for the moment, her Lytess mannerisms.

There was a charming little boy in the picture, Tommy Rettig. Though he was only eleven, he was thoroughly professional. Because Marilyn had so much trouble remembering her lines, we often had to do a scene about twenty and more times. Tommy Rettig delivered his lines perfectly, every time.

One morning Tommy seemed upset. He could not remember his lines. He could not follow my direction. Then he started suddenly to sob. I called his mother to the set and she explained that the night before Miss Lytess had talked to Tommy during dinner. She told him that most child actors lost their talent unless they took lessons. She offered her services and said: "You must learn to use your instrument."

I barred her from the set. "You can be with Miss Monroe in her dressing room if she wants you there," I told her, "but you are not permitted on the set."

Natasha had Marilyn send a telegram to Zanuck, threatening to quit the picture. Zanuck, in turn, sent me a long wire listing all the favors he had done for me in the past. Monroe was money in the bank for Twentieth Century-Fox, he pointed out. He could not take the risk of her quitting. I must permit Natasha on the set. I had no choice. Natasha returned to the set but she had alienated the whole cast and crew when she upset Tommy Rettig. Everyone in the company cut her dead. She sat huddled on a stool, ignored by everybody except faithful Marilyn, who was putty in the hands of fakes like Natasha Lytess.

# 23

## REQUIEM FOR A FATHER

After *River of No Return*, I decided not to work ever again as a studio employee. I paid Fox $150,000 to cancel my half-year contract. I sold my house in Bel Air and settled in a New York apartment. I returned to California, where I kept an office, only occasionally on business and to see my parents and my brother.

My father was sixty-one years old when he arrived in America —too young to retire but too old to go through legal training all over again in a new language.

He cast around for something to do. For a short time he played with the idea of settling all the Premingers on a farm, but he changed his mind soon after I expressed my lack of interest. He decided instead to invest the modest amount of money he had brought with him in the stock market.

He didn't approach anybody for advice. Instead, he studied the histories of various corporations, read their annual reports, and analyzed trends. He was a thorough and intelligent man. When he completed his research and started to invest his money his decisions were sound. He was wealthier when he died than when he had arrived here. In the meantime, he had lived well for over fourteen years, buying a house for himself and one for my brother as well.

He was seventy-five years old on January 15, 1952, when we

gathered beside my mother's bed to celebrate. She had been almost completely paralyzed by a stroke ten years earlier. My father knew then that he was dying of cancer. He never spoke of it. His doctor suggested that he might prolong his life if he submitted to surgery, but he would have none of it.

He wasted away quickly. Once when I visited him he was too weak to fasten the buckle on his wristwatch. I bought him an expansion bracelet, which pleased him, but soon it was loose on his thin wrist. He died on the eighth of February, 1952.

I buried him with a heavy heart but I often think of him as though he were still alive. When I'm about to make a decision or something interesting or amusing happens, I am tempted to reach for the telephone and call him. Sometimes I have a conversation with him in my mind, putting to him some thoughts and concerns and imagining his loving and wise counsel.

I try to relate to my children as he did to me. He never attempted to change my mind once I had made a decision. I thought privately that my son Erik's marriage was a mistake; they were too young. But I kept silent as my father did when I married Marion Mill. When they divorced I didn't say I had expected it; neither did my father say that to me.

After my father's death my brother Ingo and I were concerned that my mother would not be able to bear it. He had visited her every day in the nursing hospital where she lay helpless. But the human will to survive is never to be underestimated. She endured the grief and hung on to living. My brother's wife, Kate, behaved beautifully. She had three young children but she found time to visit my mother every day. She brought her gifts, food or flowers or perfume and, most important, her warmth and love. She was my mother's steadfast comfort for the remaining years of her life.

# 24

## BLACK IS BEAUTIFUL

Oscar Hammerstein wrote a revue, *Carmen Jones,* which Billy Rose produced on Broadway in 1943. A black cast performed skits which were loosely based on the opera *Carmen.* The score by Bizet was simplified and changed so that the performers who had no operatic training could sing it.

I was fascinated by the idea of transposing the story of *Carmen* into present-day American life with an all-black cast. I engaged Harry Kleiner, who had been one of my students at Yale, and started to work with him on the screenplay. Except for the lyrics, we did not use the text of Hammerstein's revue or the libretto of the original opera by Meilhac and Halévy but went back to the original story by Prosper Mérimée. For I had decided to make a dramatic film with music rather than a conventional film musical. I was also going to use the original score, eliminating only the recitatives.

I went to see my friends Arthur Krim and Robert Benjamin at United Artists and submitted the project to them. I expected them to share my enthusiasm, particularly as *The Moon Is Blue* had become the first big hit of their management. But they were rather quiet when I finished and asked me for time to think it over and discuss it with their associates. A few days later they took me to lunch at "21" and tactfully explained that they could not take the risk of backing an all-black film. "Sorry, Otto," they said, "but this is too rich for our blood." They pointed out that pictures like *The Green Pastures* and *Cabin in the Sky* had failed at the box office. I could do anything else I liked for them but not this. I soon discovered that most other companies would not touch it either.

I was editing *The River of No Return* at the Fox Studio in Hollywood when Zanuck called me to his office. He had heard through the grapevine about my difficulties with *Carmen Jones*. "Have you a script?" he asked. "Can I read it?" Two days later he called me again and offered to finance the film. I was surprised. Twentieth Century-Fox had hardly ever backed an independent producer. Zanuck picked up the phone and called on his direct line Joseph Moscowitz, the vice-president in charge of business affairs at the home office in New York. He told him about our conversation and asked him to negotiate the deal with me. Moscowitz protested shrilly over the loudspeaker on Zanuck's desk. He said that the money was as good as lost if they went ahead with such a crazy project. Zanuck paid no attention. He made an appointment for me to discuss the contract with Moscowitz in New York.

I went to New York. Moscowitz's master plan was to stall until I gave up. He said he needed an itemized budget. When I submitted it, he kept finding flaws and asked for more particulars. He wanted a complete script. I gave it to him. Then he said he had to straighten out some details with a lawyer. It went on for months, during which I finished *The River of No Return*.

Zanuck was in Paris. I took the rough cut of the film to him. He looked at it and liked it. "How is *Carmen Jones* coming along?" he asked. "When are you starting?"

I was glad he had asked. "I don't know when I'm starting," I told him. "I can't get a contract. Moscowitz keeps promising that it will be ready tomorrow, and tomorrow he says it will be ready next week, and next week he says in a few days. But it is never ready."

Zanuck's famous temper flared. He grabbed a telephone and called Moscowitz. "Joe," he thundered, "you will be on the next plane to Paris. You will bring with you the necessary papers and sign that contract with Preminger right here."

Moscowitz arrived two days later. He admitted that he had hoped I would give up. He didn't believe in the picture. He thought it was pure folly. In fact, he continued to resist it. He would give me no more than $750,000, an almost impossibly low budget for a musical. I accepted.

I cast the leading roles with Harry Belafonte, a night-club singer who had never made a film, and Dorothy Dandridge, a former child actress whose reputation was confined to night clubs as well. Even though both were singers, they were not able to sing an operatic score, so I auditioned young singers, most of them still in school, to record the songs. Marilyn Horne, who has since become an opera star of world-wide repute, was just a teenager when I picked her to lend her voice to Dorothy Dandridge. Today she is the most acclaimed Carmen.

Diahann Carroll, also a teenager then, took a supporting role, and so did Pearl Bailey. Everyone but Pearl synchronized their lip movements with the prerecorded voices of the trained singers. In her case the singing part was within reach of her voice. Though the prerecorded voices presented technical problems, we had to shoot the picture in four weeks in order to stay within Moscowitz's budget.

*Carmen Jones* was among the few of my pictures that succeeded with both the critics and the public. Its triumph was proof of what I had tried to explain first to Krim and Benjamin and then to other doubting executives like Moscowitz. There are no rules like "pictures with black actors won't make money." Just because black films hadn't made money in the past it didn't mean that they would not in the future. A good story is a good story, even if a similar one failed in the past. A good actor is still a good actor, even if he has given a bad performance recently. And a good director remains a good director, even after making several unsuccessful pictures. There is no formula for success. You cannot play safe by mixing two parts of sex, two parts of violence, a few tears, and two dozen laughs. Even when a film is finished and acclaimed by critics it is impossible to predict its success at the box office. I follow my personal taste, my instinct. If I feel enthusiastic about a story, its theme, its characters, I put it on the screen as I see it and hope to transfer my enthusiasm to the audience. If I succeed, word of mouth is my ally. But my real reward is my work itself. Success matters only because without it one cannot continue to work.

I made *The Man with the Golden Arm* right after *Carmen Jones,* and this time United Artists stood behind me. They went so far as to resign from the Association of Motion Picture Producers and distributed the picture, which was condemned because of an arbitrary clause in the code that forbade even the mention of narcotics.

In 1957 I was in California when Sam Goldwyn called me. He told me he had just fired Rouben Mamoulian, who was supposed to direct *Porgy and Bess,* and asked me to take over.

I read the script and asked for changes. Goldwyn agreed. I inspected the sets, which were more suited for a stage production than a film. I wanted them changed and Goldwyn agreed. I demanded three weeks of rehearsals before shooting. Goldwyn agreed. I wanted to do part of the picture on location. Goldwyn said that was all right with him.

My brother Ingo acted as my agent in the contract negotiations. He and Goldwyn agreed on the salary but couldn't get together on the participation arrangement. Goldwyn was offering 10 per cent of the profits and Ingo asked for 50, my usual share. Goldwyn wouldn't budge. I became impatient. "Look," I said to Ingo, "let's leave it to Goldwyn. When the picture is finished and he sees it he can decide what my percentage should be."

Goldwyn was surprised and promised to be fair. He thanked Ingo warmly and I proceeded with the picture. My fights with Goldwyn began immediately after I started. They became the talk of the studio. People used to gather under the open window of my office to hear me bellow at him on the telephone.

In calmer retrospect, I see that much of Goldwyn's curious behavior was due to the fact that he didn't understand the technical side of film-making. He was a showman with a great instinct, but cameras and other mechanical equipment completely baffled him.

He called me one day on location after he had seen the dailies. "The rushes don't match," he complained.

"Of course they match," I told him. "They must match. What do you mean?"

He asked me to come in. Though this was inconvenient, be-

Don Murray, Charles Laughton, Walter Pidgeon, and Otto, *Advise and Consent*, 1962 (COPYRIGHT © ALPHA-ALPINE S.A. A COLUMBIA RELEASE)

Charles Laughton and Otto, *Advise and Consent*, 1962 (MARK SHAW)

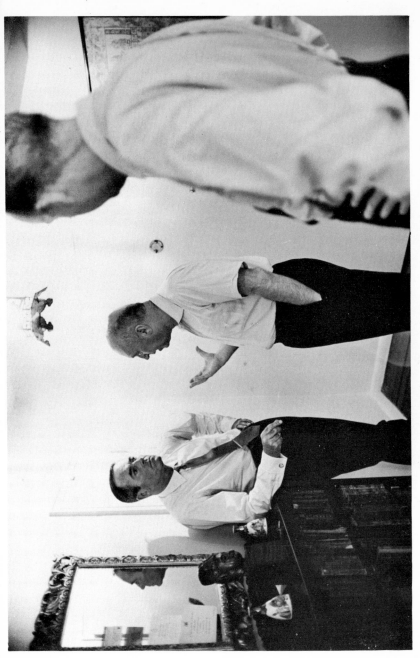

Henry Fonda and Otto, *Advise and Consent*, 1962 ( MARK SHAW )

Senator and Mrs. Henry Jackson, Otto, and Gene Tierney, *Advise and Consent*, 1962 (COPYRIGHT © ALPHA-ALPINE S.A. A COLUMBIA RELEASE)

cause we were some distance away, my cameraman and friend Leon Shamroy sacrificed his Sunday and drove with me to Goldwyn's house in Beverly Hills. We saw the rushes and they were perfect.

"Why did you say that the rushes don't match?" I asked Goldwyn.

He snickered. "I just wanted to see if you know what you're doing."

One day Goldwyn came to the set and told me he had seen the dailies and the photography was beautiful.

"Tell Shamroy," I suggested.

"Why should I?" asked Goldwyn. "I pay him enough."

Another day he informed me that he liked the rushes but hoped we would use more light in the other version.

"The other version?" I said, puzzled.

"The 35mm version," he explained. "I saw them in 70mm."

"There is no other version," I said.

"What am I going to do!" he began to wail. "Most theatres can't play 70mm. If you don't make a 35mm version most theatres won't show the picture."

I tried to explain: pictures shot in 70mm are printed down in the laboratory to 35mm. You don't have to shoot two versions. He couldn't grasp it. I took him to Shamroy, who went through it again. Goldwyn was still moaning about "the other version." Finally he called the laboratory and they confirmed that it was the method universally used.

Some of the performers in *Porgy and Bess* had worked with me in *Carmen Jones*. Dorothy Dandridge again played the lead, this time opposite Sidney Poitier. Sammy Davis, Jr., Pearl Bailey, Brock Peters, Diahann Carroll, and Roy Glenn played important roles. There were a great number of smaller parts and the chorus. I introduced myself to the entire cast before rehearsals started. "I want you to know that I grew up in Europe. For me there is no difference between black and white people. So if you behave badly I will be just as tough with you as I would be with white actors."

Rehearsals, I added, would start on Monday morning.

Sammy Davis, Jr., spoke up: "I won't be here on Monday."

"Why not?" I asked.

"It's Rosh Hashanah," he explained. "It's the Jewish New Year."

I said, "I'm Jewish too, Sammy, and I'll be here on Monday."

"There's a difference," he replied. "You're an old Jew, I'm a new Jew."

One night after we had spent the day rehearsing the scene in which Crown, played by Brock Peters, rapes Bess, Dorothy Dandridge called me.

"Otto," she said, sounding very upset, "you must recast him. I can't stand that man."

"Dorothy, are you out of your mind? You're not casting the film, I am. I think Brock Peters will be very good in the part. I know he's not ready yet, but you're not perfect either in everything you're doing." She got more upset. She kept saying she couldn't work with him. "When he puts his hands on me I can't bear it," she cried hysterically. It went on for about fifteen minutes, at the end of which she exclaimed, "And—and—and he's so black!"

I calmed her down and Peters continued in the part, but her tortured "he's so black" revealed to me the tragedy of Dorothy Dandridge. She was divorced from a black man who had fathered her retarded child. From then on she avoided black men. For her love affairs she always chose white men.

She had been bitterly poor in her youth and one of the great fears of her life was poverty. She lived frugally and saved every cent she could. Some years after we made *Porgy and Bess* she called me and asked if I would be her guest at the opening of a new restaurant in Hollywood. I went and she introduced me to the owner, a tall, handsome white man with white hair and particularly beautiful narrow, white hands. He was about fifty years old. "We're in love," she told me happily.

They had met in Las Vegas, where he had been a maître d'hôtel. They planned to be married. "Did you invest money in this restaurant?" I asked. She laughed. "You know me. You know I wouldn't put money into anything."

She married that man and they spent all her money. She had to sell her house and everything of value she owned. Then he left her.

The last time I saw her she was living in a one-room basement apartment, almost penniless. She was only forty-two when she died of injuries that many people think were the result of a suicide attempt.

Ingo got in touch with Goldwyn after *Porgy and Bess* was finished. "You remember that we left the matter of Otto's profit participation up to you," he reminded Goldwyn. "The picture is finished now and we are wondering what you have decided."

Goldwyn replied, "You left it to me?"

Ingo: "Yes."

Goldwyn: "You left the participation to me. So there is no participation."

He was giving me a sample of one of his often-quoted Goldwynisms: "An oral promise isn't worth the paper it's written on."

When I showed the film to the executives of Columbia Pictures, which distributed it, they were full of praise, although they felt the story was too downbeat. One of them suggested that I add a last scene in which Porgy gets up and walks. Needless to say, I refused.

# 25

## SERGE RUBINSTEIN AND OTHER FIGHTS

Serge Rubinstein came to see me in California during the summer of 1937 with a letter of introduction from my father. He was the son of the Czar's last banker, who had fled Russia during the Revolution and settled in Vienna. His father bought a house in Vienna with the proceeds from the sale of diamonds his wife had smuggled across the border by concealing them in her hair and other parts of her big body.

Serge was sent to study economics at Oxford. After he graduated with all possible honors he asked the dean for a letter of introduction to some Swiss banks, where he wanted to continue his studies and eventually become a banker. The letter opened many doors and enabled him to pull off a daring scheme. He knew that many Russian aristocrats, who were among the richest people in Europe, had kept their money in Swiss banks. Most of them had been killed during the Revolution. Their accounts were dormant, with no deposits or withdrawals over a period of years. Using his access to the banks, Rubinstein made a detailed list of those dormant accounts. He then went to Paris and carefully selected, one at a time, Russian refugees living in poverty there. He briefed them carefully how to impersonate relatives of the dead aristocrats and claim their accounts. He provided each one with affidavits and a skilled lawyer. According to Swiss law the banks had to advertise for six months in the newspapers that there was a claimant to the account. If no other heir stepped forward the money was turned over to the fake relative, who shared it with Rubinstein. Because Rubinstein's name never appeared during this procedure, he could repeat it over and over again. Thus he obtained several million Swiss francs.

Rubinstein was ugly, short, and fat but he could be charming when he exerted himself. One Sunday he was at a luncheon in my house in Beverly Hills. In order to impress a young French actress, he talked at the table a good deal about his success and his money. He had just returned from Japan with suitcases full of cash and a beautiful sable coat.

The following Sunday he was again my guest at lunch. This time he related that he had tricked the French actress into going to bed with him. He took her out to dinner and afterward showed her the sable coat, implying that he would give it to her in return for her favors. In front of my other guests he crowed: "Can you imagine that stupid little French bitch? She really expected me to give her the expensive sable coat that I bought for my mother."

I asked him to leave my house immediately and never to return.

Many years later he stopped me on the street in New York. "Look," he said, "I know I was wrong and behaved badly, but after all these years please forgive me and let's be friends again." He had just bought the house at 814 Fifth Avenue from the estate of Kitty Miller's father, Jules Bache. He invited me and my wife to dinner there and inquired what I was doing. I told him I was working on a new play. He said he wanted to invest in it. The production was all capitalized, but he persisted and I sold him a percentage of my own share for five hundred dollars.

The play opened in Philadelphia and didn't do well. One evening I was standing at the back of the half-empty theatre when I saw Serge, wearing his inevitable black Homburg, coming up the aisle.

"Serge," I said, "why didn't you let me know you were coming? I would have arranged for tickets."

He said he happened to be in town and wanted to see the

play. It wasn't too promising, I advised him. He made no comment.

A few days later I received a letter from his lawyer. Rubinstein wanted his money back. He had conceived of a legal loophole. Rubinstein's check was drawn by the City Investment Corporation, which he owned, and his lawyer claimed that under the law a corporation cannot be a partner in a limited partnership.

I consulted my lawyer, Sol Rosenblatt, whose language became colorful. When he calmed down he wrote Rubinstein's lawyer a curt letter to the effect that, according to law, when a mistake is made the party who made the mistake cannot use it to his own advantage.

Rubinstein really wanted to be friendly with me, but he couldn't resist his greed for a petty five hundred dollars. About a year later Rubinstein was found murdered in his own bed. Neither the motive nor the identity of his killer have ever been discovered.

I have observed on several occasions that wealthy businessmen will court show business personalities because of their so-called glamour. They want to have them attend their parties and show them off to their friends.

Nathan Cummings, one of the wealthiest men in North America, called me one day. He introduced himself and said he was giving a party for Baron Edmond de Rothschild and hoped I would be able to attend. I couldn't remember Edmond de Rothschild at first, but then I recalled that he had given a party in Paris to celebrate the world premiere of my film *Exodus*. I accepted the invitation.

The party took place in Cummings' big apartment at the Waldorf Towers, where tables for ten had been arranged. There was an attractive woman of about thirty-five seated next to me. She told me that she had two children and her husband wanted a third. She agreed to it on the condition that he would permit her to choose another man to father the child.

"I'm looking around," she told me calmly. I was stunned. I didn't know whether I was expected to offer my services as stud. One meets strange people at New York parties.

I was planning another film about Israel based on a book by

Dan Kurzman, *Genesis 1948*. Cummings learned of it. He called me and offered to finance it. I advised him that the budget was about five million dollars, but he wasn't in the least discouraged. He would sell twenty shares of $250,000 each to his friends, he said. I was to stop any efforts I was making elsewhere for financing. He would look after it.

Naturally I was pleased to be relieved of that problem. I instructed my lawyers to get in touch with Cummings. Time passed and it turned out that Cummings was finding himself too busy to sell shares. He would take one share himself, but that was all he was prepared to do.

He committed himself in a letter to my lawyer and I thought the matter was settled. A month later Cummings wrote me that he had come to the conclusion that his role in society was in the arts and not in films. He would not be taking the share after all. I could have sued, I suppose, but I didn't want to be bothered.

I saw Cummings a week later at a party I attended in another rich man's apartment. Cummings came up to me and greeted me warmly. "Hello, Otto! How are you?" he said, extending his hand.

I looked at it. "You don't think I will touch your hand?" I said. "Why?" he asked, seemingly surprised. "Try to find your own answer," I said, and walked away. But Cummings followed me, grabbed my arm, and asked, with an innocent smile, "You're not mad at me, are you?" Well, I could not resist the temptation and slapped him twice across the face, right in front of his rich friends and their overdressed wives.

There was only one encounter in my life that involved bloodshed, and the blood was all over me. I had been negotiating the purchase of the film rights to Truman Capote's *In Cold Blood*. I was led to believe that the property was mine, so I was dismayed to discover that Capote's agent, Irving Lazar, had sold it instead to Richard Brooks.

Soon afterward, Lazar and I were at adjoining tables at "21." I made some comment and he said furiously, "If you're going to talk like that, I'm leaving."

I did not try to dissuade him. He got up with his drink in his hand and started to move toward another table, but suddenly he turned around and broke the glass over my bald head. Blood poured out, covering my face and soaking into my clothes. I could hardly see, but I struggled to my feet and started after him. Waiters held me back while someone called the police.

My poor wife was shocked and frightened as the police drove me to a hospital, where a plastic surgeon closed the cuts with fifty-one stitches. Luckily the glass didn't cut my eyes.

Lazar was charged with felonious assault.

He eventually wrote me a letter of apology and I withdrew the charges.

# 26

## SOME LOVELY PEOPLE

The camera demands reality and registers without mercy everything artificial. That's why a real room looks better on the screen than a set, even if it is an exact replica of that room. That's why the stage actor is at a disadvantage on the screen. Laurence Olivier, one of the great actors of our time, has, despite his good looks and many excellent performances, never become a popular film star. Certainly you admire him or Helen Hayes or Tallulah Bankhead on the screen. You admire their talent, their style, but you never forget that they are acting. You don't identify with them.

I made only one film with Gary Cooper: *The Court-Martial of Billy Mitchell*. Cooper was a great film star. Nobody will dispute that. But during our work together I discovered that he was also an actor. In fact, the actor Cooper created the film star. The slow, hesitant speech and movement, the downward look, the so-called shit-kicking were invented by him in order to face the camera with a semblance of the complete reality that the medium demands. In life he was different, a charming, witty, intelligent, and entertaining companion appreciated by men and adored by women.

In 1954 I had completed *Carmen Jones* but had not yet started *The Man with the Golden Arm*. Milton Sperling, a producer-writer at the Warner Brothers Studio sent me the script of *The Court-Martial of Billy Mitchell* and asked me to direct it.

Emmet Lavery, the author of *The First Legion*, the last play I directed in Vienna before coming to America, worked on the Billy Mitchell script with Sperling. I felt it could be improved and suggested Ben Hecht for the polish job. The filming was supposed to start on a Wednesday and Hecht was meeting with Sperling and me the Sunday before at my home. I outlined the changes I wanted, which were considerable. Hecht was known to be the fastest writer in Hollywood but I felt that it wouldn't be possible, even for him, to meet the deadline. "Please do as much as you can before we start shooting. I realize that you cannot finish the whole script." "Sure I can if you just get me some Demerol," was his answer. Milton Sperling, Gary Cooper, and I contacted our doctors and requested a prescription for Demerol. In each case the answer was: "You want it for Ben Hecht and I won't give it to you." Hecht had had surgery a year earlier and got hooked on the drug.

Hecht was one of the most interesting men I ever met. He had a wonderful original wit which he never turned against anyone with malice. He was also a person of uncompromising principle. In the years before the founding of Israel he backed the anti-British Jewish underground so openly and forcefully that Great Britain banned all pictures with his name in the credits. It cost him a great deal of money but it didn't deter him from supporting the Irgun.

Hecht had a strange marriage. He treated his wife with polite but impersonal deference, like some stranger he never expected to see again. He adored his daughter and perhaps for that reason never sought a divorce. It annoyed him that his wife encouraged the child to become an actress. Hecht could think of no worse fate. As it happened, she tried acting for a time but was not successful.

Hecht had a long relationship with a Hungarian beauty. Eventually it ended and she wrote him a letter which implied that she would inform his wife of their affair if Hecht did not pay her a large sum of money. Hecht had his lawyer send a formal reply which stated that Ben Hecht's finances were handled by Mrs.

Hecht and that any request for money should therefore be directed to her.

I learned a great deal from Hecht about writing. He was not only very fast and usually superb but also took criticism without the least sign of stress. Most writers respond in one of two ways when asked to change what they have written: either they put up a fight and insist it is fine the way they did it or they claim what you want done is impossible.

For Hecht nothing was impossible. He considered himself an employee who was delivering a product on order.

Pauline Kael once said that Hecht wrote half of Hollywood's most entertaining movies, and it is true that his productivity probably will never be catalogued. Because he wrote so quickly he thought it was better if his name did not appear too often in the credits. His facility as a screenwriter came in part from his contempt for the profession. He really felt that film work was beneath him. But he couldn't resist the money. He was the first writer in Hollywood to be paid a thousand dollars a day. If Ben Hecht had not been sidetracked by films, he would most probably have become one of the greatest playwrights of all time.

Sperling, the producer of *The Court-Martial of Billy Mitchell*, was a nice man but he was uncertain of his judgment and kept changing his mind. Every day he countermanded the orders he had given the day before and issued new ones, which he would rescind the next day. This made our work difficult and caused endless confusion.

Féfé Ferry became a quite successful agent in Hollywood. As he grew older, he came to see the emptiness of an existence that depended so frantically on invitations to parties and famous or rich people waving hello to him. He met a charming young aspiring actress. They lived together for almost two years. Then they decided to give up her career and his freedom. The wedding was to take place in Düsseldorf, West Germany, where a sister of the bride lived. They invited me to attend. I was about to leave for Düsseldorf when she telephoned me: "Féfé just died of a heart attack." He was a dear man.

Charles Laughton is another friend I miss greatly. We met in 1960 when I cast him in *Advise and Consent*. I learned a great deal from him. As an actor he left nothing to chance. He went to

Washington several weeks before we started rehearsals there. He visited Senator John C. Stennis, who, like the senator Laughton was to play in the film, came from the Deep South. He watched him on the Senate floor for weeks and asked him to read the part into a tape recorder. Then he listened to the tape until he mastered the accent to perfection. Watching his preparation I thought Laughton would probably not need or want direction from me. Instead, he asked for it and paid close attention to my suggestions. We became instant friends. When he was interviewed and asked if I was really as tough as my reputation would have it, he used to answer: "Nonsense! He is pure mush!"

A few months after the picture was finished, Laughton called me in the middle of the night. He was touring the Midwest with his one-man show of readings. He had slipped in his bathtub and hurt his hip. He tried to be admitted to a hospital in Chicago but there were no beds. Could I perhaps help? I persuaded him to come to New York instead, where I booked a room in the New York Hospital. After ten days of tests the doctors ruled out the possibility of cancer. Hope and I went to see him and found him weeping uncontrollably with relief. We drank a bottle of champagne together and celebrated.

Eventually Laughton returned to California. After a few weeks Burgess Meredith, one of Laughton's closest friends, called me. He had just learned that Charles indeed had cancer. I went to see him in Los Angeles. He did not recognize me any more.

# 27

## CASTING ABOUT

In 1956 I decided to make a film of George Bernard Shaw's *Saint Joan*. I have had an almost lifelong love affair with that play. I read it first in German when I went to school in Vienna and later directed it with great success at the Theater in der Josefstadt. I know every line of it, but I was to discover, too late, after I had released the film, that I had not understood something fundamental about the play. In casting the film I had to face the problem that Saint Joan was little more than a child at the time of her death. In the theatre, the distance from the audience makes it possible for mature actresses to create the illusion of youth. However, for the film I needed an actress who actually was young but had enough understanding of the play's intellectual concept to interpret the part. I therefore announced that I would audition young actresses all over the United States and Europe and asked the United Artists offices in all big cities to handle the preliminary interviews. The talent hunt for Saint Joan became perhaps the most publicized and extensive one in screen history.

Some eighteen thousand teenagers and young women who looked like teenagers were auditioned. Out of that vast number about two thousand seemed promising enough to be auditioned by me personally. I went from city to city over a period of eight exhausting weeks and saw them all.

When I directed the Swedish star Bibi Andersson in Peter Stone's adaptation of Erich Maria Remarque's *Full Circle* on the New York stage in the fall of 1973, she described to me how excited she was when I arrived in Stockholm for the audition. She was all prepared, had even her hair cut short, but Ingmar Bergman, to whom she was engaged at the time, did not permit her to audition for me.

United Artists had rented a ballroom in Chicago for about three hundred contenders from the Midwest. One of them was the daughter of a druggist from Marshalltown, Iowa. Her name was Jean Seberg. She was seventeen years old and had no professional experience whatever. She read for me and I was impressed. I asked her to come with her parents to my hotel and we made a contract. A number of other young women seemed very talented, but she appeared to have the strength and simplicity that I wanted.

From time to time I meet some of the many losers in that talent hunt. Almost ten years later I was looking for a ten-year-old boy to play a part in *Hurry Sundown*. I visited a public school in New York. After showing me around, the principal told me that her secretary was anxious to meet me. We went to her office and as soon as we entered a small, elderly woman got up from behind a desk and started to berate me. "My name is Streisand," she said. "I am Barbra Streisand's mother. I just want to tell you that my daughter auditioned for *Saint Joan* and you did not give her the part." Her voice was rising. "You, a famous director! And you didn't recognize talent when you saw it."

I tried to calm her and said soothingly, "My dear Mrs. Streisand, please, compare your daughter's career with Jean Seberg's. You should be grateful I didn't cast her as Saint Joan. It might have ruined her future."

John Gielgud, in my opinion the greatest living actor, played Warwick in *Saint Joan*. He is also one of the most charming men I know, with an engaging sense of humor. On the first day of filming, after I had finished a scene with him and Anton Walbrook, he took me aside and asked cheerfully, "Well, how does it feel to direct two old aunties?" Noël Coward was also frank about his homosexuality and comfortable with it long before the Gay Liberation Movement. In 1964 he played a part in my film

*Bunny Lake Is Missing* and we remained friends until his death.

During the filming of *Saint Joan* all of us, cast and crew, were carried by our enthusiasm. The dailies looked excellent. The photography by Georges Périnal, one of the all-time great cameramen, was beautiful. But during the world premiere at the Paris Opéra and afterward, at a lavish party at Maxim's, while being the center of enthusiastic praise and congratulations, I started to realize that my film *Saint Joan* was a failure.

Many people blamed Jean Seberg and her inexperience. That is unfair. I alone am to blame because, as I said before, I misunderstood something fundamental about Shaw's play. It is not a dramatization of the legend of Joan of Arc which is filled with emotion and religious passion. It is a deep but cool intellectual examination of the role religion plays in the history of man. And I realized later that even the most successful stage productions of *Saint Joan* were not commercial hits. Katharine Cornell's celebrated Saint Joan carried the play just barely through a hundred performances in New York.

Am I sorry I made the film? No. For I loved working on it. I met another delightful man through the picture: Graham Greene, who did the screenplay. He is a great writer and a delightful companion. Though he gives a first impression of being controlled, correct, and British he is actually mad about women. Sex is on his mind all the time.

When Graham Greene read this, he wrote me an amusing note protesting: "This sentence doesn't seem quite fair to me. If it were true, I would not have written so many books."

We had an interesting time together in London but he kept telling me, "Wait until we get to Paris. I know a stupendous place there. You have never seen anything like it in your life."

On our first evening in Paris, Greene hurried me into a taxi. "The lady who runs this establishment has amazing resources," he explained to me. "You can go to any show in Paris and if there is a girl you fancy you have only to make a note of her. For instance, you tell the madame that you want the fourth dancer from the left and she will be delivered to you right after the show."

I made no comment when he gave the taxi driver the address

of the extraordinary establishment. We arrived and were admitted to a lavishly furnished anteroom. Graham Greene prepared to introduce me to the madame as she entered but before he could do so she rushed past him and embraced me. "Monsieur Preminger!" she cried. "How wonderful to see you again!"

When I was preparing *Anatomy of a Murder* I had difficulty casting the role of the judge. I offered it to Spencer Tracy, who turned it down because it was not an important enough part for him, and even Burl Ives rejected it. My assistant, Nat Rudich, had a suggestion: "Let's use a real judge, like, for instance, Judge Learned Hand." I had never heard of Judge Learned Hand but it gave me an idea. "I wonder if we could persuade Joseph Welch to do it?" I said.

Joseph N. Welch was a Boston lawyer who represented the Army during the McCarthy Senate hearings and became the hero of American conscience. McCarthy wanted to discredit Welch but he was above suspicion so he singled out a young lawyer who assisted Welch and accused him, without proof, of Communist leanings. Welch turned to McCarthy: "Have you no sense of decency, sir?" he asked him. I had seen this scene on television and with millions of others had become an ardent admirer of Welch, who was one of the major forces in the defeat of McCarthyism.

I called Welch in Boston and asked if he would consider playing a judge in a film. He agreed to look at the script. I sent it to him by special messenger and two days later Joseph Welch appeared in my New York office. He walked around, leisurely inspecting the furnishings, my desk, which is a huge slab of white marble, the black leather chairs, the windows with their white vertical blinds, and the large modern paintings on the walls.

"Did you read the script, Mr. Welch?" I inquired.

"No," he replied, like a real actor, "I read only my part."

"Do you want to do it?"

"Naturally I want to do it."

So we made a contract. During rehearsals I remembered an episode which I witnessed during my apprenticeship with Max Reinhardt. I watched him rehearse a scene in a play by the Czech dramatist Karel Čapek. It took place in a pub. Reinhardt instructed an actor to enter, hang up his hat, and say, "Good evening." Like Welch, the actor was not a professional. He was Reinhardt's friend Egon Friedell, a great philosopher and writer who from time to time played a small part just for the fun of it. Friedell, who was a huge man, came to the footlights and asked: "What shall I do first, Professor, hang up my hat, or say, 'Good evening'? "Do it simultaneously," was Reinhardt's answer. "Oh, if you want that you must get yourself a real actor." He was right. The ability to coordinate movement and speech makes the difference between the professional actor and the amateur. I was very careful while directing Joseph Welch never to make him move and talk at the same time. With that small assistance he gave an excellent performance which was widely acclaimed. He brought to the role a reality that no actor could have matched. I gave his wife a ringside seat from which to watch her husband by making her one of the jurors. We filmed *Anatomy of a Murder* in Ishpeming and Marquette, two small communities on Michigan's northern peninsula, the home of the book's author. He was a retired judge, John Voelker, who used the pseudonym Robert Traver. I worked on the script with Wendell Mayes, who later wrote the screenplay for *Advise and Consent* and *In Harm's Way*.

My first choice for the female lead was Lana Turner. Hope Bryce, my costume coordinator and later my wife, selected a pair of slacks in a Beverly Hills shop and asked Lana to meet her there in order to try them on. Miss Turner failed to appear. Her agent, Paul Kohner, called me. He explained that his client's wardrobe was as usual to be designed by the fashionable Jean Louis. I pointed out that she was to play a second lieutenant's wife in the film and the selected outfit was correct. Besides, I, and nobody else, determine what the actors wear in my films. Kohner said: "Sorry, she won't do it." "Fine," I said, "send me a letter stating that she would like to cancel her contract unless her clothes are designed by Jean Louis. I will release her immediately." Kohner knew that Columbia was anxious to have Lana Turner star in the film and assumed I was bluffing. He sent the letter and I released her. When the Columbia executives learned about it they were very upset. They even offered me to pay Jean Louis' salary without charging it to the picture. I refused and signed Lee Remick, who became a star with the part. *Anatomy of a Murder* did the same for George C. Scott and Ben Gazzara. Jimmy Stewart gave one of his best performances and won a prize at the Venice Festival. He is not only a brilliant actor but a rare man on a personal level as well. I haven't seen him for several years but I feel close to him, as though we had finished working on the film yesterday. The outstanding cast included Arthur O'Connell, Eve Arden, Orson Bean, the Chicago talk-show host Irving Kupcinet, and Duke Ellington, who wrote the score.

Our presence created great excitement in those little towns. The special train carrying cast, crew, and equipment arrived at six-thirty on a March day, but half the population was at the station to greet us. Duke Ellington arrived a few days after we had begun to shoot. Usually the producer waits until the filming and the first cut are completed, then he chooses the composer, who writes the score in about six weeks. I find it useful to have the composer with me on the set. By watching the progress of the shooting, seeing the dailies with me, discussing the music daily, he becomes part of the film. This system eliminates most well-known, sought-after composers because they are not willing to devote all that time to one picture. Therefore, most of my films were scored by newcomers like Herschel B. Gilbert (*The Moon Is Blue*), Elmer Bernstein (*The Man with the Golden Arm*), Ernest Gold (*Exodus*), and Jerry Goldsmith (*In Harm's Way*). Duke Ellington was willing to sacrifice his valuable time and work according to my system. I also gave him a role in the film. He played the pianist in a roadhouse and enjoyed the experience hugely.

Ten years later, in 1969, about eight weeks after the inauguration of President Richard Nixon, I arrived in my office in the morning and started to open my mail. The first letter was a "thank-you note" from Senator Hubert Humphrey, whom I had supported in his unsuccessful campaign for the presidency. The second envelope contained an invitation for dinner from the President and Mrs. Richard Nixon. I called Hope and said: "This must be a strange joke somebody is playing on us. Why should Nixon invite us? We don't know him and we didn't vote for him. Lyndon Johnson, whom we got to know well while he was senator and we were filming *Advise and Consent* in Washington, took several years after becoming President before he invited us to a rather boring state dinner for the Prime Minister of New Zealand and Nixon invites us to the White House after only eight weeks." "Well," my darling wife answered, "he is probably desperate for guests." In fact—I learned later—it was a party to celebrate the seventieth birthday of Duke Ellington, whose father (or grandfather) had been a servant at the White House. The Duke had put our names on the guest list.

Because we had filmed *Anatomy of a Murder* in Michigan we decided to open the picture with a charity premiere in Detroit. The governor gave a dinner and led a parade through the streets of the city. About half an hour after the performance had started my assistant, Nat Rudich, called me out of the theatre. He had just received a call from Chicago. The picture was scheduled to open there the following day. It had been viewed by the censorship board, which demanded five cuts.

I took the next plane to Chicago. It did not improve my mood when the captain announced shortly before arrival that the landing gear was stuck and we might have to make a belly landing. He suggested that we remain calm and we circled for about two hours. Finally, the gear went down and so did we. The office of film censor in Chicago was held by the chief of police. He was too busy to see the pictures himself and was advised by a board of twelve women, all widows of policemen who had lost their lives while on duty. The chairman of this advisory board was a former chauffeur of the mayor who had to retire from driving because of failing eyesight.

I went to see the police chief, a very handsome, tall man with white hair. Before I could say a word he began: "I've heard of you, Mr. Preminger. They tell me you are very tough. My board suggests five cuts, but I will compromise. I will settle for just one." "And what is the cut you want, sir?" I asked, although I had no intention of giving in.

"They tell me that there is the word 'contraceptive' in your film," he said. "I would not want my eighteen-year-old daughter to go to a movie and hear that word."

"If I had an eighteen-year-old daughter, sir, I would teach her that word and explain to her carefully all about it."

He didn't think much of my suggestion. "The film won't be shown unless you cut that word," he said coldly.

I appealed to the court the next morning. The judge asked to see the film in the afternoon. "Would you mind if I bring my wife and my two sons?" he asked.

When I saw his sons, who were ten and eleven, I knew we would have no problem with that judge. He saw the film and said to me, "I will order the chief of police to pass the film without cuts."

There are references in *Anatomy of a Murder* to rape and seduction, either of which might offend a censoring board such as Chicago was using. But the police chief was Catholic and the word contraceptive seemed to him intolerable. The film had no difficulty anywhere else.

*Advise and Consent,* which I made in 1961 after I finished *Exodus,* had a cast of wonderful performers: Henry Fonda, Charles Laughton, Burgess Meredith, Lew Ayres, a quiet man who hadn't been in a film for a long time, Franchot Tone who also had been out of films for more than a decade, Peter Lawford, Walter Pidgeon, a newcomer George Grizzard, who was just beginning his successful career, and Gene Tierney, making a comeback attempt after her serious mental breakdown.

The casting had gone much as I had hoped, with one exception. I wanted the civil rights leader Martin Luther King, Jr., to play the role of a senator from Georgia. I wanted to demonstrate that a black man could be creditable in such a political situation. Dr. King was intrigued but at the last moment declined. He decided that the hostility his presence would create in that role would jeopardize his cause.

Allen Drury's book *Advise and Consent* had a complicated plot about some unpleasant wheelings and dealings in Washington. It wasn't critical of the American political system but of the men who hold high office and abuse it. It was both prophetic and understated, as Watergate demonstrated almost twelve years later.

Nevertheless, at the time it was considered in some quarters practically an act of treason. There were complaints that making a film about misbehaving politicians constituted a sinister attempt to overthrow the government.

I was convinced that just the opposite was true. The fact that we could make the picture in Washington with the cooperation of the government, even shooting some scenes in Congress itself, proved that our system was sound and strong. This country's tolerance of free expression is its greatest asset. I believed that the picture would show the world that liberty isn't an empty word in America.

When the film was finished, Senator Young of Ohio rose in the Senate and announced that he would introduce a bill preventing Columbia Pictures from distributing *Advise and Consent* outside of the United States. He declared that it would do irreparable harm to the prestige of America abroad.

I had advance warning of his proposal and had taken a negative out of the country to prevent confiscation in case his bill was successful. I was determined to show the film and show that he was wrong.

His bill came to nothing, but I did prove my point. One of the largest newspapers in France, *Le Monde*, ran a front-page story marveling at the freedom of America. Though France is not a dictatorship, there is heavy government censorship of political ideas in films. *Le Monde* commented that it was impossible for a film such as *Advise and Consent* to be made or shown about the French government.

All over Europe journalists praised the American government for cooperating in the making of the film and allowing it to be distributed freely.

Years later, there was a retrospective of my films in Paris and I met with some students from the Sorbonne. They were obsessed with the fact that the film had been made in Washington with the government's knowledge and participation. Their reaction made me proud of my American citizenship all over again.

I remember the cast of that film appreciatively, mainly because it introduced me to Charles Laughton, who became a close friend. A highlight of the shooting, however, was provided by Burgess Meredith. He gave one of the greatest performances I have ever seen in the short but important role of Herbert Gelman, a witness who lies. I didn't direct him, he did it all himself.

On the other hand, my film *Tell Me That You Love Me, Junie Moon*, which I made in 1969, had a cast that was quite different from the Hollywood Who's Who that appeared in *Advise and Consent*. The film was based on Marjorie Kellogg's touching story of three young people with physical afflictions, one of them a girl whose face is horribly burned. I offered the part to Liza Minnelli. She had done only two films at that time, one of them not yet released, but she was my first choice.

The other young people were males, and I signed for one of the roles Robert Moore, who had never acted before. He is a gifted director who had two stage successes, one off-Broadway, *The Boys in the Band*, and one on Broadway, *Promises, Promises*. He came to me to ask if he could play a small part in one of my films because he wanted to watch me work. He wanted to become a film director, which he eventually did. While we talked, I began to think that he might be able to play one of the leads in *Junie Moon*. We made a test and I signed him.

The other male lead was played by Ken Howard, also a newcomer to films but with some acting experience. I had admired his performance in the Broadway musical *1776*, in which he played Thomas Jefferson. James Coco, a dear friend whom I also had started in films, played another role.

Somehow those four people became a family. They really cared about one another in much the same way as the characters they were playing. Shooting that film was a pure pleasure, except for the tragic death of Judy Garland, Liza Minnelli's mother. It happened while we were rehearsing and I naturally offered to excuse Liza. She refused, though it fell on her shoulders to make all the arrangements for the funeral. She was only twenty-three at the time but behaved with great maturity. She asked for only one concession: that we rehearse in her house so that she could take care of the funeral details and avoid the press.

Judy Garland had asked that all her children attend the funeral and she had left instructions about how she was to be embalmed and that she wanted her favorite Hollywood makeup man to do her face.

Liza undertook to follow her mother's last wishes to the letter. I offered to help out by contacting the makeup man in California. I tracked him down and found that he worked for Eva Gabor on the television show *Green Acres*. He would miss only one show if he flew East and did Judy's makeup. He was willing

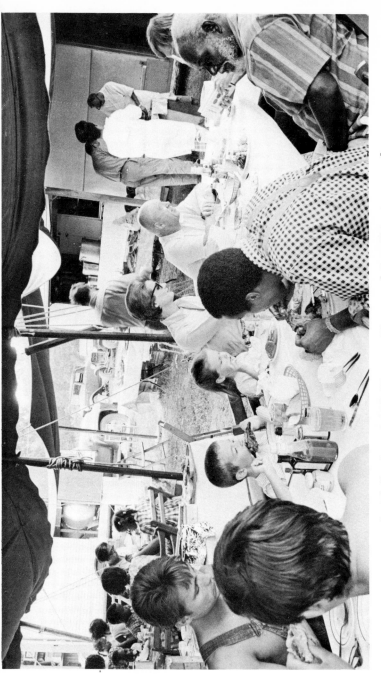

John Phillip Law, Mark, Victoria, Hope, and Otto Preminger, and Robert Hooks (checked shirt) on location (*Hurry Sundown* COPYRIGHT © MCMLXVI BY SIGMA PRODUCTIONS, INC. ALL RIGHTS RESERVED, STILLS FURNISHED BY PARAMOUNT PICTURES CORPORATION)

Carol Lynley, Keir Dullea, Laurence Olivier, and Clive Revill, *Bunny Lake Is Missing*, 1965 (COPYRIGHT © 1965 WHEEL PRODUCTIONS LIMITED)

Ken Howard, Liza Minnelli, Hope and Otto Preminger, *Tell Me That You Love Me, Junie Moon*, 1970 (LEO MIRKINE)

Robert Moore, Otto, James Coco, Ken Howard (*Tell Me That You Love Me, Junie Moon* COPYRIGHT © MCMLXIX BY SIGMA PRODUCTIONS, INC. ALL RIGHTS RESERVED. STILLS FURNISHED BY PARAMOUNT PICTURES CORPORATION)

and we obtained the permission of the show's producer. He only asked me, as a courtesy, to clear it with Eva Gabor.

She said no.

Liza accepted it with dignity. I hope her life works out well. She is a great woman and I believe even more talented than her gifted mother.

There is no place in the casting of a film or play for selecting a performer wholly on the basis of compatibility or friendship or shared political views. There is probably no star whose politics are more at variance with mine than John Wayne's, but in 1964, when I was looking for a U. S. Navy captain type for the film *In Harm's Way*, I had no hesitation asking John Wayne to do it and he had none in accepting it.

On the morning of the first day of shooting on location in Hawaii my driver gave me a magazine of extreme reactionary views, which he said John Wayne wanted me to read. He had marked a column in it for my attention.

I put it aside without reading it. When I saw Wayne later in the day I said, "Look, John, anybody over thirty has made up his mind about politics. You know where you stand politically and I would never succeed in converting you. I would not even try. So you shouldn't try to convert me to your opinions. Let's agree not to talk politics and we'll get along very well."

And we did get along well. Wayne is an ideal professional: always prompt, always prepared. He is also humorous. At the end of the shooting the governor of Hawaii gave a party for the cast. My wife Hope and I were in the receiving line and I presented each guest with a lei of red flowers. When Wayne got his he grinned at me. "Now at last you are showing your true colors," he said.

The good timetable that we kept in the making of *In Harm's Way* helped to save John Wayne's life. We finished ten days ahead of schedule and Wayne used the free time to have a medical checkup. It was discovered that he had lung cancer. The doctor requested to see the X-rays that were taken twelve weeks earlier when Wayne was examined for the usual cast insurance. It turned out to everybody's surprise and shock that the cancer showed on those X-rays too, but had not been noticed.

On the other end of the political spectrum, I cast Jane Fonda in *Hurry Sundown,* which we made in the Deep South in 1966. At that time, however, she was not the angry radical she later became. She was wholly absorbed by love for her husband, the director Roger Vadim, who accompanied her to Louisiana.

Vadim is a man of such charm that I had the feeling he had put the same concentration and skill into the development of his personality that others put into their professions. Jane Fonda adored him and I can easily understand why many actresses have loved him and been desolate when he moved on.

He behaved with exquisite tact during the shooting of *Hurry Sundown.* It can be quite unpleasant for a director to have another director watching his every move, but I personally didn't mind, so I invited him to come to the set when Jane was working. He declined politely, saying it was not the proper thing for him to do and stayed away throughout.

It is a different matter when a director is on the set because he has switched roles and become an actor. When I am acting for another director in my standard Nazi parts, I do as I am asked and make no suggestions.

When I was casting *The Cardinal,* there was the part of Cardinal Glennon that needed a character actor. I didn't want to use any of the established character actors because they would bring too much of their familiar image to the role. I wanted someone new, but also impressive, and it occurred to me that John Huston would be perfect.

He had never been in front of a camera before. I found him in London and took him to lunch.

"I have a part that you must play," I said.

"You must be out of your mind," he protested. "I'm not an actor. I wouldn't dream of playing it."

We talked for hours before I wore him down enough to agree to come with me to my hotel and read the script. We read the part together and when we finished he looked at me thoughtfully.

"Okay," he said. "I'll do it."

He has played many roles since.

Huston was a joy to direct. He behaved as we both want actors to behave: he came to the set on time knowing his lines. He rehearsed and did the role without the slightest critical comment about the direction or even a hint of professional advice. Perfect.

I appeared on a weekly talk show that John Lindsay used to conduct when he was mayor of New York. I asked him if he planned to run again and he said he had decided against it. "When you stop being mayor I'll give you a part in one of my pictures," I promised. In 1974 I made the film *Rosebud*. There was the part of a United States senator. Remembering Lindsay's political ambitions and my half-serious invitation, I decided to offer it to him. We traced him to where he was vacationing in Europe. When we did reach him he seemed to have been influenced by stories of the astronomical fees some stars claim to receive.

I persuaded him that his price was unrealistic and we settled for a more reasonable amount. I suspect that good politicians can switch to acting without effort. I would vote for John if he ran for office again, or offer him a part in a film any time I had one that suits him.

# 28

## EXODUS AND ALL THAT

In the fall of 1958 I was spending a few days with my brother Ingo in California. I saw an untidy pile of cardboard boxes filled with manuscript pages and I asked what it was.

"It's a very interesting novel written by one of my clients, Leon Uris," he told me.

"Why didn't you show it to me?" I complained. "Here you are my brother and an agent and you know I'm always looking for properties."

"I couldn't show it to you," he said. "It belongs to MGM. Metro commissioned Uris to write a book about the founding of Israel. They want to make a picture about Jews who had to fight their way to Israel on a ship called *Exodus*. You can read it if you like, but it isn't available."

I started reading it after dinner and couldn't put it down. I sat up most of the night and when I finished I knew I wanted to make that film. I asked Ingo for the details of Uris' contract with Metro. He said it was an outright buy of the film rights for $75,000.

I couldn't get the book out of my mind. As soon as I returned to New York I went to see the president of MGM, Joseph Vogel, and said I wanted to save him a lot of money—$75,000 to be exact.

"What do you mean?" he asked.

"You own a book by Leon Uris about the exodus of the Jews to Israel but you'll never produce it. I'm here to take it off your hands."

He said, "That's crazy. Of course we shall produce it. Everyone tells me it is a great book."

"It is," I assured him, "but if you make it the Arab countries will close all MGM theatres and ban all MGM films. You can't afford an Arab boycott but I can. Since I am an independent producer, they can't hurt me too much."

He wasn't impressed. He told me smilingly that there wasn't a chance that MGM would let me have *Exodus*, but if they changed their minds he would certainly get in touch.

However, he was worried enough to mention it at the next Board meeting. The seed I had planted began to bloom. The possibility of an Arab boycott was very real and MGM had property and profits to protect.

Vogel called me a week later. "If you still want to buy it," he said, "we're ready to make a deal. How much are you offering?"

"It cost you $75,000," I replied, "so I'll pay you $75,000."

He was shocked. "After all," he said, "we commissioned the book. It was our idea from the start."

"Yes," I agreed, "but you can't produce it."

Metro sold me the film rights to *Exodus* for $75,000 and I went to Arthur Krim of United Artists for production money. He was interested in Israel: his wife, Mathilda, was a research scientist at the Weizmann Institute. He agreed to back me for a budget of three and a half million.

I began to work on the script with Leon Uris. We labored through almost a third of it but it was hopeless. Like Nelson Algren, Uris is a good storyteller but cannot write a screenplay. Somerset Maugham, who was both a novelist and a dramatist, once said that whenever he dramatized one of his novels he changed and rewrote every line of dialogue. Dialogue to read, he explained, is very different from dialogue to hear. Uris and Algren kept returning to the dialogue of their novels. In a film or play it is the dialogue which must tell the entire story. In the novel the narrative does part of the work.

I have had some well-publicized battles with writers. Nelson

Algren wrote about his conflict with me in a book and Leon Uris went from talk show to talk show with complaints about Preminger. The record will show, however, that many writers worked well with me. Wendell Mayes wrote several scripts for me and we are still good friends. I usually work daily for several hours with the writer until the script is finished. Some directors who do this get a writer's credit, and they are entitled to it, but I never have. To me, it is part of my job as director. Just as I direct the actors, the scenic designer, the set decorator, the editor, I consider it my job to direct the writer.

When I paid Uris off and discharged him from *Exodus* he was furious. When the film was released he declared publicly that I had ruined his book. About ten years after the picture was finished I met him at a dinner President Lyndon Johnson gave in the White House. I have a habit of forgetting unpleasant experiences. So I put out my hand and said, "Hello, Leon, it's nice to see you. How are you?"

He looked at me coldly and turned his back to me. He is still mad. I am sorry, but I have not lost much sleep over it.

I tried to finish the *Exodus* script with Albert Maltz, who was blacklisted and lived in Mexico. Maltz was impressive to watch. Whenever I visited him I found him surrounded by tables piled high with research material he was collecting. But he never got around to writing a line.

Much time had been wasted and I was in a desperate hurry. I turned to Dalton Trumbo, who, like Ben Hecht, was fast and facile. Trumbo was one of the Hollywood Ten, working under various pseudonyms to get around the studio blacklist.

I moved into the Beverly Hills Hotel and began a schedule of rising at six every morning to drive to Trumbo's house in Pasadena. We worked in a cottage apart from the main house. He showed me whatever scene he had just written and while I worked on it he wrote another one, then did the suggested revisions on the first scene. Then I studied the second while he worked on a third, and so on.

Around five-thirty in the afternoon he used to mix himself a martini and after a few sips he was too relaxed to continue working.

It took forty days to finish the script to my satisfaction. I told

Trumbo that I was going to break the boycott against him and give him screen credit under his real name. He didn't believe it could be done, but I succeeded and the days of the blacklist were finally over.

I wanted Paul Newman for the role of Ari Ben Canaan, the young Hagannah officer who sails the shipload of Jewish refugees to Israel. His agent was Lew Wasserman, who has since become head of Universal Pictures. He came to negotiate with me and asked for $200,000.

"That's too high," I said. "I'll give him half."

"Fine," he said without hesitation. "It's a deal."

I often repeat that exchange when my dealings with agents become complicated by endless bargaining. Wasserman didn't haggle nor did he say that he had to consult his client. The part was good for Newman and he wanted him to do it and that was that.

I had admired Eva Marie Saint in her first film, *On the Waterfront*, for which she won an Academy Award. I signed her for the role of the American nurse.

I cast my friend Gregory Ratoff in a small but juicy part that he relished.

There was a role in *Exodus* for a very young girl. I auditioned dozens of them, a parade reminiscent of the search for Saint Joan, but this time involving girls who were almost children. Finally I selected Jill Haworth, who was only fourteen years old.

I was astonished when I read recently that she appeared nude in a London play. I still think of her as a child.

The completed script of *Exodus* was likely to annoy both the British and the Arabs, but I soon discovered that the Israelis were not entirely happy with it either. They wanted nothing in the script that was unflattering to Israel. In my opinion that would have been unrealistic. Drama is not the expression of one individual's opinion: drama is created by the presentation of opposite points of view, giving each of them fair value.

I don't believe in villains anyway. If someone is a villain I try to find out why. I don't necessarily excuse him, but I try to understand him.

My insistence on impartiality got me into trouble in Israel. The government graciously gave a reception for me, where I met

Prime Minister David Ben Gurion, Golda Meir, who was then Minister of Foreign Affairs, and General Moshe Dayan, all members of the ruling Labor Party. They told me they were disappointed. They thought the script gave too much credit to the extremists—the Irgun and the Stern Gang—for the creation of Israel.

I said politely that I didn't think Israel would have emerged as a nation without the terrorists. I don't like violence but that is unfortunately the truth. The British would never have given in without the high pressure from the radical element.

The Israelis were not convinced. They asked if I had to show the bombing of the King David Hotel and the prison break in Acre, which were credited to the Irgun. I pointed out that those were matters of historical record. But they were still displeased.

It turned out that the radicals, too, felt that I had been unfair to them. The day before we were to shoot the film's biggest scene, the one near the end where thousands of people gather in the square to cheer the proclamation of the state of Israel, I was invited to have lunch with the leader of the Opposition Party, Manachem Begin. He started the conversation by saying, "Mr. Preminger, you do not give us enough credit in your script."

"How did you get a copy of the script?" I asked. "I didn't give it to you."

"Never mind," he said. "We know that you are shooting the big scene tomorrow night and we are going to picket you."

"That's fine," I said. "I'll photograph you and your pickets. You will all be in the film."

They didn't show up.

I next met Begin in Brussels in March 1971, where I had agreed to attend the World Conference on Soviet Jewry. The sessions took place in a large hall and I was given a seat on the podium, with some other so-called "names."

Suddenly there was a flurry of excited movement on the floor. Rabbi Meir Kahane, the radical leader of the Jewish Defense League, had arrived uninvited and requested to speak. He was refused. He then asked if he could sit in the audience with his friends and listen to the proceedings, but that was also refused. The conference organizers called the police. The police took the hint and found something wrong with his passport and deported him.

I was so outraged that I went to the microphone and gave an angry speech. "Russia couldn't have a greater triumph," I said, "than to see that this organization, which supposedly wants to work for Russian Jews and their freedom, acts unfair and discriminatory against a rabbi."

My point was that whether or not we agree with Rabbi Kahane and his violent methods—and I personally do not—we owe him the courtesy to listen to him.

The audience downstairs was extremely hostile to my speech. But soon hundreds of young people rushed down from the gallery and gave me an ovation.

Twice I have been able to intervene on behalf of Soviet Jews.

In 1962 I was invited to Russia by the Union of Soviet Picture Makers, which paid all expenses for a ten-day trip for me and my wife and arranged a number of receptions and gatherings in my honor.

To return the hospitality, I invited the union to select two young directors to come to America at my expense. It turned out that the two chosen were the president of the film-makers union, Pirieff, who was at that time about sixty-eight years old, and the vice-president, a younger man, Lev A. Kulidzhanov, who has since succeeded him.

I was shooting *The Cardinal* at the time and I offered them a choice of the film's locations: Rome, Vienna, Boston, or Hollywood. They picked Hollywood.

Because of my good relationship with the Russian film-makers, the Israeli consul in New York asked me a few years later to help two Jews who wanted to leave the Soviet Union. One was a famous director, Mikhail N. Kalik, whose film *Man Follows the Sun* I saw while in Russia. It was a beautiful film: the story of a boy who plays with several friends on the roof of a building. They look at the sun through colored glass. An older boy tells him: "If you follow the sun you will eventually come back here." The boy starts out and the film tells his adventures, shows the people he meets, the places he visits, and what he learns on the trip.

Kalik had applied for permission to emigrate to Israel. He had been refused and, in addition, was expelled from the union of picture makers.

I sent union president Kulidzhanov a long cable, asking him either to help a colleague leave Russia or to take him back into the union. Two weeks later I had a call from Paris. Kalik had arrived with his whole family. He then settled in Israel, learned Hebrew, and has already finished his first film there.

The Israeli consul then asked me to help with another case, this one a film writer. I used the same channel and it worked again.

During the filming of *Exodus* and, later, of *Rosebud* in Israel, I received full cooperation everywhere. One of the most helpful people was Meyer Weisgal, a man I had met when I was Max Reinhardt's assistant at the Salzburg Festival during the summer of 1924.

Weisgal was not only Reinhardt's friend and admirer, he was the one who raised the money for some of his staggeringly expensive productions. He secured backing for Reinhardt's *The Eternal Road*, which played in the now-vanished Manhattan Opera House.

To Weisgal's dismay, Reinhardt was even more extravagant than usual. He had Norman Bel Geddes design such huge sets that they couldn't be brought in through the stage entrance and the wall had to be broken. It was a familiar rhythm: every other day Reinhardt would be struck with an inspiration and order something wonderful for the production, disregarding the budget. Weisgal would then raise another $50,000 to cover it, by which time Reinhardt would have spent more.

While waiting for the curtain to rise at one of the last dress rehearsals, Reinhardt turned a disapproving eye on the seats in the theatre.

"The red velvet looks shabby," he commented. "I think we should have the seats recovered."

His yes-men all agreed.

"What do you think we should cover them with?" Reinhardt asked.

One suggested blue silk, another thought chintz would be nice.

Reinhardt turned to Weisgal, who was in pain.

"What do you think we should put on the seats, Meyer?"

"Asses, Professor," he moaned, "*asses*."

Weisgal later founded the Weizmann Institute of Science in Rehovot, named for Chaim Weizmann, the Zionist leader who became the first President of Israel. Weisgal had been Weizmann's secretary for many years.

Through the offices of Weisgal, all doors in Israel were open to the *Exodus* company. We were given assistance by the mayors of Jerusalem and Haifa. Weisgal even played a small part in the film, portraying Prime Minister Ben Gurion. Because of our friendship, the world premiere of *Exodus* took place in New York for the benefit of the Weizmann Institute. Tickets for the film and the dinner afterward sold for four hundred dollars each and the Institute realized a substantial amount of money. In addition, I donated all the income from the Israeli distribution of the film to the Weizmann Institute.

Weisgal was delighted and went around telling people that he had been paid a million dollars for his role in *Exodus*.

# 29

## CRITIC'S CHOICE AND CHOICE CRITICS

Twenty-five years after my first Broadway play, *Libel!* opened I presented *Critic's Choice* by Ira Levin at the Ethel Barrymore Theatre. The play was well received and ran for 189 performances. Warner Brothers bought the film rights and cast, or rather miscast, Bob Hope in the leading part, which Henry Fonda had played on the stage to perfection. It was then and still is a strange Hollywood phenomenon that they hardly ever let the original cast repeat their roles when filming a play. After the sensational success of Laurette Taylor in *Outward Bound* on the stage, they starred Gertrude Lawrence in the picture, which was a failure because she was wrong for the part.

Henry Fonda is a most professional actor, a joy to work with. Beyond that, he exerts a very healthy influence on the whole cast. Usually actors take small liberties and make some changes during a long run. Not Fonda. About four months after the play had opened he called me one day and asked if he might, in a certain scene, sit down two or three lines later than we had agreed during rehearsals. If the star is that conscientious, the other actors follow suit. Therefore the last performance of *Critic's Choice* was exactly as precise and fresh as the premiere.

As was to be expected, some critics were unable to refrain

from making remarks about the play's title which were meant to be witty.

I have the reputation of hating critics because I had some overpublicized run-ins with a few of them. Nothing could be further from the truth.

The fact that educated men and women study our work and evaluate it seriously is most important, regardless of whether or not we agree with them. Critics like Vincent Canby, Clive Barnes, Walter Kerr, Kathleen Carroll, Arthur Knight, Pauline Kael, Douglas Watt, and Archer Winsten, to mention just a few, are an integral part of theatre and film and equally as important as directors, actors, and producers. However, I exclude from this appreciation the so-called critics who try to make a name for themselves by passing off glib wisecracks and create artificial controversy. Rex Reed is an example of that type. He is a special enemy of mine. When he published his list of the Ten Best and Ten Worst films of 1973 he added a note that, to his regret, there had been no Otto Preminger film released that year. Therefore he had none for the Rotten classification. I could only laugh. Reed is a frustrated little man who wanted to become an actor but couldn't make it. I met him first in 1965 while I was directing *Hurry Sundown* in Baton Rouge. He was unknown then and had been assigned by the New York *Times* to write a story about the making of my film. I made him welcome and even gave him a small part, which delighted him. When he left he thanked me and said the most flattering things about my work. When his article appeared in the Sunday *Times* it was full of the grossest misstatements and described me as a ruthless tyrant. I don't remember the details except that he told how I fired the cameraman, Loyal Griggs, in a moment of uncontrolled fury. The truth was that he had to quit because of a back injury and kept on working in spite of pains until his replacement arrived from California. I was not troubled by his lies, but Griggs, through his lawyer, demanded and received a retraction from the New York *Times*. It also had its funny side. Reed quoted Michael Caine as saying that I was paranoid. Caine cabled the *Times:* "I did not know what the word meant so I looked it up and I can assure you, paranoid he is not."

Toward the end of 1968 I appeared with the critic John Simon on a Dick Cavett TV talk show. He gave his list of the year's Ten Best and Ten Worst films. Among the worst, he listed Stanley Kubrick's *2001: A Space Odyssey* and Peter Bogdanovich's *The Last Picture Show*. I pointed out that those were very successful films and appeared on most critics' Ten Best lists. "You don't understand," he answered. "I don't write for now. I write for the future. In fifty years you will see how right I was." "Mr. Simon," I said, "I don't expect to be here in fifty years. But I have a suggestion for you: instead of publishing your reviews now, put them all in a sack and bury them. In fifty years dig them up and have them printed."

The audience roared with laughter but Simon did not appreciate my suggestion.

In 1974, during the filming of *Rosebud*, I had a strange experience involving Kenneth Tynan, once regarded as the most important and intelligent British critic. In that picture Peter O'Toole plays the role of a CIA man who poses as the Paris correspondent of an American news magazine. I rented the small, book-littered apartment of an actual newspaperman, Tom Curtis of the Paris *Herald Tribune*, to serve as O'Toole's quarters in the film. The apartment was located on the second floor of the Tour d'Argent building. Curtis moved to a flat on the fifth floor that belonged to a friend of his.

When I arrived with the crew at seven in the morning to prepare for the first day's shooting, we found a letter addressed: Peter O'Toole, Personal and Confidential. O'Toole's call was for eleven o'clock. Upon arrival he opened the letter. It contained a note advising that the writing was reversed and could only be read by holding it to a mirror. It was a vicious letter berating O'Toole for acting in a film against the Palestinians, who were in the same boat as the Irish. It threatened to stop the production with violence, starting with a bomb that would explode at noon and tear the building apart. We cleared the building at once. I notified the police and Claude Terrail, the owner of the Tour d'Argent restaurant, who evacuated the kitchen personnel and the waiters who were preparing our lunch. One member of the British crew whose children had almost been killed by an IRA bomb a few months earlier had a nervous breakdown and could not stop shaking and sobbing. I noticed that Tom Curtis was not among those who had left the building. I found him upstairs in his friend's apartment and asked him if he was not scared. "It's just a joke," he told me. "I had a few friends here for dinner last night, among them Kenneth Tynan. He wrote it as a prank."

I asked him for Tynan's telephone number, as he was in Paris working on some project with a London producer.

I reached him and called him every name I could think of because I felt that particularly at a time when bombs explode daily and kill innocent people his "prank" was cruel, stupid, and vicious. Then I went downstairs to continue work. But we could not find O'Toole. As it was past noon I broke for lunch, which was served to us at the restaurant on the top of the building. About forty-five minutes later O'Toole joined me. He apologized but refused to say where he had been. Three hours later a petulant letter of apology from Tynan was delivered to me by hand. He wrote: "Dear Mr. Preminger: Today one of your employees, Peter O'Toole, has very capably beaten me up, I presume not on your instructions or with your knowledge. From his point of view the dispute has been—very audibly—settled by physical force. Like any competent secret policeman, he took care not to draw blood and aimed nearly all his blows beneath the belt. This was very unfortunate because (as I thought he knew) I have a fairly notorious hernia and the effect of having my balls repeatedly punched was to send me straight to a doctor. That I have a clear case of assault against Peter is beyond doubt."

He then explained that his letter was written as a joke, like "an apple-pie bed." He meant to give O'Toole "a start and a laugh."

He wrote: "Nobody (I thought) could possibly have taken it for anything other than a parody." He said he was genuinely sorry and added: "I suppose O'Toole could be said to have demonstrated his *machismo* ("His steel-blue eyes glinting, Sheriff O'Toole kicked the cowering Apache in the gut . . .") I am not a pugilist; in my physical condition it wouldn't pay. If O'Toole had tried to con *me*, I would have riposted in kind, and probably beaten him at his own game, because I am just conceivably cleverer . . ." And so on. I am astonished that a supposedly intelligent man could have done such a stupid thing or written such a silly letter.

# 30

## THE CARDINAL GOES TO VIENNA

*The Cardinal,* a novel by Henry Morton Robinson, had been published ten years before I happened to read it. Columbia Pictures had bought the film rights but decided not to produce the film when Cardinal Spellman attacked the book with all his ferocious energy. Spellman believed that the central character, a young priest who matures into an important Cardinal of the Roman Catholic Church, was modeled after him. He was particularly incensed because the fictional Cardinal had a sister who became pregnant, although she was not married. He maintained that this was an insult to his own sister, despite the fact that she was happily married and nothing of the kind had happened in her life. Because of Spellman's objections to the book, Columbia had shelved the picture.

I took Abe Schneider, the chairman of the Board, and Leo Jaffe, the president of Columbia Pictures, to lunch. I told them that I wanted to film *The Cardinal.* They were afraid that Cardinal Spellman's stand would hurt the picture. I reminded them that Spellman and the whole weight of the Catholic Church had been pitted against *The Moon Is Blue* and it did not matter. Finally they agreed to let me do the film.

The script presented great difficulties. Robert Dozier worked on it and received credit for the screenplay, but almost all of it was rewritten by Gore Vidal, whose name does not appear in the film's credits.

The Screen Writers' Guild once more handed down a strange and arbitrary ruling, insisting that Dozier and Vidal share the billing equally and alphabetically, although their contributions were far from equal. Vidal preferred to withdraw his name rather than be a party to such an unfair arrangement.

Something of almost identical stupidity happened ten years later with my film *Rosebud*. The script was written by my son Erik Lee Preminger. But we felt that the dialogue of the five young girls was not quite satisfactory. I contacted Marjorie Kellogg, who had written *Tell Me That You Love Me, Junie Moon*. She flew to Europe and rewrote the lines the five girls spoke. On the original prints the credits read: Screenplay by Erik Lee Preminger, Additional Dialogue by Marjorie Kellogg. Everybody was happy. Nobody complained. But the Screen Writers' Guild summoned Marjorie and Erik and gave them three choices: One: Screenplay by Erik Lee Preminger. Two: Screenplay by Erik Lee Preminger and Marjorie Kellogg. Three: the case would go to special arbitration to determine if the screen credit should read: Screenplay by Erik Lee Preminger, Adaptation by Marjorie Kellogg.

Marjorie was very gracious in this impossible situation created by the bureaucracy of the Screen Writers' Guild. She did not want equal billing or a credit that she adapted the whole script because it would not be truthful. She withdrew her name and allowed Erik to have sole credit.

Cardinal Spellman sent letters to every bishop in the United States asking them not to cooperate with me on the filming of *The Cardinal*. He would have been opposed to a film version of *The Cardinal* in any case, but he was particularly furious because I was doing it, remembering *The Moon Is Blue*. Spellman's campaign made it impossible for me to find a priest to be my technical adviser on the picture. Eventually a very charming and knowledgeable man who had left the priesthood agreed to do it. His name was Donald Hayne. The next obstacle was the impossibility of finding a church where we could film some of the scenes. Since the young priest in the story came from Boston, I contacted Cardinal Cushing. He invited me to come and see him. He had read the book and liked it. I asked him for assistance, particularly for permission to shoot in a church. He refused. He said in essence: "I am sorry but I have put up with that man in New York for the past sixteen years. I'm tired of fighting with him. He wrote me a letter asking me not to assist you. I can't give you a church. If, however, you want me to see the film when it is finished I'll be happy to view it."

When the picture was ready I took it to Boston and arranged a special screening for Cardinal Cushing. He came and brought several guests, among them Dr. Spellman, the Cardinal's brother. After the screening Cardinal Cushing congratulated me warmly. Later he wrote a rave review of the film in *The Pilot*, a Catholic publication in Boston. When I called to thank him he said he wished he could have written it for the New York *Times*. I took the cue and reprinted his review in an ad in the *Times* when the picture opened in New York.

Nevertheless, his earlier refusal to let me use a church in his jurisdiction was a serious blow. We had already prepared all the other locations for the scenes that took place in Boston. We rented a small house and furnished it in the style of the twenties; borrowed some old streetcars from a museum and dusted off railway carriages of the right vintage. Everything was ready except the church.

I was growing desperate. My assistant, Nat Rudich, a devout Jew who lived in Stamford, Connecticut, discussed the problem one day with his rabbi. The rabbi knew the pastor of the Catholic church in Stamford. The pastor loved movies. It was a long shot, but he would perhaps allow us to use the church if I asked him personally. I went to see him and found that the priest was indeed a movie buff. He had seen all my films. When I asked him the all-important question he said without hesitation: "But of course, Mr. Preminger, you can have my church any time you want to."

He was a sweet old man in his early eighties and I did not want to take advantage of him. I told him about Cardinal Spellman's campaign against the film. In that case, the old priest said, after considering it for a minute, he would have to get permission from his bishop in Springfield.

I sent Rudich to Springfield and he submitted the request to the bishop.

His answer was: "If the pastor wants to let Preminger use his church it's up to him. I received Cardinal Spellman's letter, but this is not in his jurisdiction."

It was my first lesson on the Catholic Church. I had been inclined to think of it as a monolith with tight discipline and unconditional obedience up and down the line. But I discovered that there was considerable individual freedom of action within the Church.

On the first day of shooting in the church the bishop and the old priest came and blessed the cast and crew. We had the same cooperation in Rome, despite Cardinal Spellman's exhortations to the contrary. The Pope permitted us to film several scenes in his summer residence and others in one of the most beautiful churches in Rome.

In Vienna, Cardinal Franz König gave us permission to shoot in the Cardinal's palace and in the famous St. Stephen's Cathedral. The pastor of the cathedral, however, had other ideas. He said we would have to postpone our work until after Lent, which would have ruined our whole schedule. I pleaded with him but he was adamant.

I went back to Cardinal König. "Your Eminence," I said, "you gave me permission to shoot in the cathedral but there are difficulties because of Lent . . ."

"Who said so?" he asked abruptly.

"The pastor says that—"

He interrupted again. "When do you want to shoot?" he asked.

"Wednesday."

"At what time?"

"Eight o'clock in the morning."

"Mr. Preminger," he said, "at eight o'clock on Wednesday morning the pastor will be in front of the church. He will hand you the key and you will shoot there for as long as you want to."

The pastor was there at eight and handed me the key.

I was beyond being surprised at the contradictions within the Catholic Church. In America, Cardinal Spellman had made it impossible for me to use a church in Boston, but in Rome the

Pope received me and my wife in private audience at the Vatican.

I had another example of contradiction shortly after *The Cardinal* was finished. I was walking toward my Fifth Avenue office in New York one morning when I was stopped by a priest. "You are Otto Preminger, aren't you?" he asked.

I said I was.

"I'm Lee Lubbers," he told me. "Would you lend me sixty cents? I need it to buy my bus ticket back to Omaha, Nebraska. I promise to return it."

"Father," I protested, "I'll be happy to give you more. Here are five dollars. Who knows what you might need on your trip."

He refused. He would accept only sixty cents. Since his bus didn't leave for a few hours, he came up with me to my office, where we chatted a while. Then we went to lunch at "21". I liked him. He was about forty, tall, blond, and balding. He told me that he was the head of the art department at Creighton University in Omaha.

He returned to New York a few weeks later to attend a show of his sculpture. He came to my office and repaid the sixty cents. Then he took me to lunch. On another visit to New York, he came to our house for dinner. Hope, respecting the fact that he was a Jesuit priest, asked if he would like to say grace before we ate. He grinned: "I never thank anybody for anything I haven't received yet."

He wears ordinary clothing so that he does not appear to be a priest. But he carries with him a strip of white cardboard that he puts under his collar to transform himself into a priest when the occasion requires it.

In 1966 my film *Hurry Sundown* was given a C (condemned) rating by the Catholic Church, which meant that Catholics were not allowed to see it. I was therefore surprised when Father Lubbers called me and asked if he could show it on the campus of his school, which has a faculty made up of Jesuit priests and an almost all-Catholic student body.

"I have to tell you," I said, "that the picture has been condemned by your Church."

"I don't care," he told me. "If you'll let me have the film I'll open our film festival with it."

"Look," I said, "I'll send you the film so you can screen it and decide if you want to do this."

He said, "Just send the picture and I'll show it."

He not only launched the film festival with *Hurry Sundown* but he invited me to speak to a seminar of his students about it. And the Church apparently was unruffled by his defiance.

The shooting of *The Cardinal* offered me an opportunity to put on film something that concerned me deeply: the behavior of the Catholic Church during the Nazi occupation of Austria.

I wrote into the script the story of Cardinal Innitzer's unhappy decision to cooperate with the Nazis and some other true incidents that occurred. It meant that we would spend several weeks in Vienna while filming these scenes. I did not expect that returning to Vienna would be a pleasant experience. There were reminders of friends everywhere who, less fortunate than I, had been sent to the death camps. I realized that it was foolish to be vindictive, because most people who stayed there during the Nazi occupation had no choice but to fall in with the ruling party, but the still-present affection for the Nazis was hard to swallow.

When I arrived at one of Vienna's finest hotels the manager escorted me to a large, handsome suite. He showed me around and declared, beaming with pride: "This is our best suite, Mr. Preminger. This is the apartment where Hitler stayed when he came to Vienna." I was impressed. "I hope you've had it cleaned since," I answered. But he didn't find that amusing.

Former Nazis held high positions of power and influence in Austria, and they made it as difficult as possible for me to work in Vienna.

The Minister of Education did not permit me to shoot in the National Library, which was in his jurisdiction. He made a public statement that it was not good for Austria to have the arrival of the Nazis filmed. I asked him, also publicly, why he did not do something about it in 1938.

In the northern part of Germany, Berlin, and Hamburg, where I worked several weeks in 1974 during the filming of *Rosebud,* I could detect no remnants of the Nazi period. But in Austria and Bavaria many people seem to feel that it was just unfortunate that Hitler lost the war.

My experiences in 1966 during the filming of *Hurry Sundown* in Louisiana made me realize the extent of racial prejudice in the South of the United States. The film dealt with a collaboration between a white man and a black man, played by John Phillip Law and Robert Hooks, which was an inflammable subject during that period of intense civil rights demonstrations. On top of that, I insisted that our integrated cast—which included Michael Caine, Jane Fonda, Diahann Carroll, and Faye Dunaway—share living and recreation facilities.

Nat Rudich and I were delighted to find, near Baton Rouge, a motel which would accommodate our entire company. We made arrangements with the manager for a substantial number of rooms. He was happy to get our business until I told him that some of his guests would be black. His expression showed his distress.

"I don't want some of our company put up in back rooms," I warned him. "All the rooms must be in the same area, with no difference in furnishings or anything else. That's the law now, you know."

"I know," he said, looking miserable.

He was even more unhappy when we moved in. Diahann Carroll had brought along her six-year-old child and a nurse to take care of the child when she was working. The nurse, however, was white. This reversal of the black mammy–white baby pattern came as a frightful shock to Baton Rouge.

The manager approached me soon after we had all registered. He told me that he wouldn't allow the black people in our company to swim in the motel swimming pool.

"What do you mean?" I barked at him. "This is 1966 and we have laws about integration . . ."

"No," he said firmly. "There isn't a law requiring integration in swimming pools."

I would not accept it, law or no law. "They are guests in the motel the same as we are and they will use whatever facilities the motel provides the same as we do."

The manager withdrew, but he had found what seemed to him a solution. The motel had two pools. He erected signs reading HURRY SUNDOWN COMPANY ONLY around one of them, leaving the other pool free for his other guests, who were without exception white.

It backfired, because the tourists were so anxious to see real movie stars that they ignored the sign and used our pool. Our contribution to the civil rights movement turned out to be daily swim-ins.

The citizens of the region were infuriated by our behavior and by the plot of the film, which put a black man and a white man on equal footing. They began to shoot at the tires of our vehicles. We received daily threats.

We arranged with the governor of Louisiana to provide state police, at our expense, to protect us. The governor pretended to be a liberal, shocked by the bigotry we were encountering.

While the French press was in Baton Rouge, their photographers took hundreds of pictures of the *Hurry Sundown* cast. One of these showed Jane Fonda with a charming little black boy. The photographer instructed Jane to put her hand on the child's head. She did so and then impulsively leaned down and kissed him.

The sheriff in charge of our state police detail, a man in our pay, came running, red-faced and yelling. "You can't do that!" he shouted. "You can't kiss that nigger!" The nigger was about four years old. But we were in his town so I had to take him seriously. "All right," I told him calmly, "we're not going to argue with you. I'll give you the film and you can destroy it."

I went to the photographer and said in French, "Give me a new pack of film." He caught on and made it seem as though it came from the camera. I returned to the sheriff with it and opened it up, exposing the film. *Paris-Match* published that picture of Jane kissing the black child.

One of my assistants, a gutsy Italian, refused to stay behind our protective wall of state police. He wanted to do some washing and went to a laundromat. The owner glared at him and asked if he was with the film company. He said he was. The owner ordered him to get out.

"I'm in the middle of washing my clothes," the assistant said. "I'm not leaving until I'm finished."

The owner disappeared into the back of the laundromat.

Otto and John V. Lindsay, *Rosebud*, 1975

Otto

Otto in Paris (DEJEAN-SYGMA)

Victoria, Hope, Mark, and Otto

When he returned he had a shotgun, cocked and aimed at the assistant.

"Get out or I'll shoot you," he said.

"Okay," my man replied, folding his arms and leaning against the washing machine, "shoot me."

The owner stared, then put down his gun. The assistant finished his laundry and left.

Lester Maddox, who later became governor of Georgia, owned a restaurant not far from our location. He telephoned one day and said he would like us all to be his guests at dinner. I told him that we would be delighted and we agreed on the date. When he learned that I would be bringing Diahann Carroll and Robert Hooks, Maddox canceled the invitation.

It seems that bigotry against the blacks reaches a high point over the question of eating together. In 1953, when I was casting *Carmen Jones,* I invited Harry Belafonte to discuss his part with him over lunch at Le Pavillon in New York City. On the day before the appointment I began to feel uneasy. I had never seen any black person in that restaurant.

I called the owner, Henri Soulé, a Frenchman whom I expected to have liberal views.

"I am meeting a famous singer tomorrow for lunch in your restaurant," I told him. "I just want to tell you that he is black."

There was a short pause. Then Soulé said, in a voice dripping with ice, "Mr. Preminger, anyone you bring is welcome."

I realized he didn't mean it. I canceled the reservation and told Belafonte to meet me at Sardi's instead.

Every adult American remembers exactly what he or she was doing on hearing the news of two terrible events in our history. One is the Japanese bombing of Pearl Harbor, and the other is the assassination of John F. Kennedy. By an ironic coincidence, what I was doing on both occasions was somewhat linked to the event. On the morning of the attack on Pearl Harbor I was rehearsing *In Time to Come,* a play about peace, and when the President was murdered on November 22, 1963, I was on a publicity tour for *The Cardinal.*

On November 21, I had been in Dallas. The next day I was in New Orleans, answering questions about *The Cardinal* at a press conference, when Roger Caras, the Columbia press representative traveling with me, interrupted. He carried a small portable television set. He was pale and told us Kennedy had been shot and was wounded. He turned on the set. Most of the newspaper people left. A few stayed. We listened until, finally, his death was announced.

I canceled whatever it was that we had planned to do that afternoon. Caras and I went out and walked aimlessly through empty streets. I felt the same grief other Americans were feeling, but in addition there was a personal loss. I had known Jack Kennedy for seventeen years as a young, vigorous, bright, and charming man.

# 3 1

## A FINAL MARRIAGE

While I was preparing the production of *Exodus* in Israel, my divorce from Mary Gardner became final and I was free at last to marry Hope Bryce. There exists no civil marriage in Israel. Only people of the same faith can get married in a religious ceremony. Since I was Jewish and Hope Episcopalian, we had planned to fly to Cyprus and get married there. But when the mayor of Haifa, Abba Koushi, heard about it he told me: "You are going to be married right here, my friend!"

"But Hope is not Jewish," I answered.

"Never mind," he said. "If the rabbis don't marry you they won't get another cent from the city of Haifa as long as I am mayor."

He made a deal with them. They knew Hope was not Jewish but pretended not to know. A marriage license is granted by a panel of three rabbis. As Hope had no papers to prove that she was Jewish, my friend Meyer Weisgal volunteered to appear as our witness. When the rabbis asked him if he knew Hope, he answered, "Of course, since she was born." "Is she Jewish?" they asked. "Absolutely," he answered.

Eleven years later Meyer wrote his autobiography under the title *Meyer Weisgal . . . So Far.* He could not resist telling the story about our marriage. The rabbis were furious. As the mayor of Haifa had died, they launched an investigation and subpoenaed Weisgal to testify. While this was going on, I was planning to go to Israel on business. I called my lawyer, Arnold Weissberger, and told him to make arrangements for me to get married. He was shocked. "To whom?" he asked. "To my wife, of course," I reassured him. A clerk of the court came to my office on the twenty-eighth of December, 1971, and married Hope and me with our eleven-year-old twins present. We toasted the occasion with champagne and that same night I flew to Israel. When I arrived in Tel Aviv a crowd of reporters bombarded me with questions about my disputed marriage. "I am very grateful to your rabbis," I answered, "for twelve years of marital bliss, but in case they should change their minds I took the precaution of getting married again in New York yesterday afternoon."

I had scheduled for the third of October, 1960, at 10 A.M., the first showing of *Exodus* for the executives of United Artists at the Capitol Theatre on Broadway. At six o'clock Hope woke up with birth pains and I hurried her to the hospital. We had been told about six weeks earlier to expect twins. The doctors at the hospital advised me that there was no point in my waiting around as the birth might not take place for a long time, so I went to the Capitol Theatre. In the middle of the screening I received a message to return to the hospital at once. When I arrived I was told that I was the father of a boy and a girl and was shown, in incubators, two tiny, curled-up bundles. I fell in love with them immediately. We called the twins Victoria and Mark. Our affection for them is a great bond between us. Hope has worked on all my pictures as costume coordinator from the time we met. She has a unique relationship with our daughter, Vicky. They talk and laugh and quarrel like contemporaries. They even wear each others' clothes.

Mark had a traumatic experience in December 1973, when he was just thirteen years old. He was riding his bicycle in Central Park when a young man stopped him, threatened him with a knife, and took his bicycle. Mark went to the police call box and reported the crime. The police showed him approximately eight hundred photographs. He identified the mugger, who was arrested, and the bicycle was recovered. I was worried when I had to tell Mark that he was to testify in front of a Grand Jury.

But he said he knew it was his duty to cooperate. I was not allowed to enter the Grand Jury room and saw my little son disappear behind a big door. When he returned he told me that he had prepared a speech to ask for mercy for the man who had taken his bicycle but he had had no opportunity to deliver it. "There was no judge," he said, very disappointed. "There was only a district attorney."

When the district attorney, a young woman, came out she said to me: "Your son is the best, most logical witness I have ever known."

When he was nine years old, Mark expressed his desire to become a doctor. When we asked him why, his answer was: "Because I want to help people."

He still wants to become a doctor. For the same reason.

*To be continued—*
*God willing.*

# OTTO PREMINGER'S STAGE PRODUCTIONS

(In Austria)

1925 KREIDEKREIS (*The Chalk Circle*)
Written by: Klabund

1931 VORUNTERSUCHUNG (*Preliminary Inquiry*)
Written by: Max Alsberg and Otto Ernst Hesse

1931 REPORTER (*The Front Page*)
Written by: Ben Hecht and Charles MacArthur

1933 DIE LIEBE DES JUNGEN NOSTY (*The Love of Young Nosty*)
Written by: Koloman von Mikszath

1933 MARKART
Written by: Duchinsky

1934 MEHR ALS LIEBE (*More than Love*)
Written by: Ladislaus Bus-Fekete

1934 CHRISTIANO ZWISCHEN HIMMEL UND HÖLLE (*Christiano Between Heaven and Hell*)
Written by: Hans Jaray

1934 MACBETH
Written by: William Shakespeare

1934  DIE PRINZESSIN AUF DER LEITER (MEINE SCHWESTER
UND ICH) (*My Sister and I*)
Written by: Louis Verneuil
1934  SENSATIONSPROZESS (*Libel!*)
Written by: Edward Wooll
1934  EINEN JUX WILL ER SICH MACHEN
Written by: Johannes Nepomuk Nestroy
1934  MENSCHEN IN WEISS (*Men in White*)
Written by: Sidney Kingsley
1935  ADRIENNE AMBROSAT
Written by: Georg Kaiser
1935  EINE FRAU LUEGT
Written by: Ladislaus Fodor
1935  DER KÖNIG MIT DEM REGENSCHIRM (*The King with
the Umbrella*)
Written by: Ralph Benatzky
1935  KLEINES BEZIRKSGERICHT (*The Little District Court*)
Written by: Otto Bielen
1935  DIE ERSTE LEGION (*The First Legion*)
Written by: Emmet Lavery


(In the United States)

1935  LIBEL!
Written by: Edward Wooll
Starring: Colin Clive, Ernest Lawford, Lewis Dayton,
Joan Marion
1938  OUTWARD BOUND
Written by: Sutton Vane
Starring: Laurette Taylor, Vincent Price, Alexander Kirk-
wood, Morgan Farley
1939  MARGIN FOR ERROR
Written by: Clare Boothe Luce
Starring: Bramwell Fletcher, Sam Levene, Otto Prem-
inger

1940  MY DEAR CHILDREN
Written by: Catherine Turney and Jerry Horwin
Starring: John Barrymore, Dorothy McGuire, George
Reynolds

1940  BEVERLY HILLS
Written by: Lynn Starling and Howard J. Green
Starring: Helen Claire, Clinton Sundberg, Violet Heming

1940  CUE FOR PASSION
Written by: Edward Chodorov and H. S. Kraft
Starring: Doris Nolan, Clare Saunders, Thomas Coley,
Claire Nielsen

1941  THE MORE THE MERRIER
Written by: Frank Gabrielson and Irvin Pincus
Starring: Louis Hector, J. C. Nugent, Dorrit Kelton, Her-
bert Duffy

1941  IN TIME TO COME
Written by: John Huston and Howard Koch
Starring: Richard Gaines, Nedda Harrigan, Randolph
Preston, William Harrigan

1951  FOUR TWELVES ARE 48
Written by: Joseph Kesselring
Starring: Rosetta Le Noire, Pat Crowley, Billy James, Jane
Du Frayne

1951  A MODERN PRIMITIVE
Written by: Herman Wouk
(Play not presented in New York)

1951  THE MOON IS BLUE
Written by: F. Hugh Herbert
Starring: Barbara Bel Geddes, Barry Nelson, Donald Cook,
Ralph Dunn

1953  THE TRIAL
Opera by Gottfried von Einem, based on *The Trial*
by Franz Kafka
Starring: John Druary, Norman Treigle, Edith Evans,
Émile Renan

1958  THIS IS GOGGLE
Written by: B. Plagerman
(No performances on Broadway)
1960  CRITIC'S CHOICE
Written by: Ira Levin
Starring: Henry Fonda, Georgann Johnson, Eddie Hodges, Murray Hamilton
1973  FULL CIRCLE
Adapted by Peter Stone from a play by Erich Maria Remarque
Starring: Bibi Andersson, Leonard Nimoy, Josef Sommer

# OTTO PREMINGER'S FILMS

(In Austria)

1931 DIE GROSSE LIEBE
Screenplay: Siegfried Bernfeld and Arthur Berger
(Based on a true story)
Starring: Hansi Niese, Attila Horbiger

(In the United States)

1936 UNDER YOUR SPELL
Screenplay: Frances Hyland and Saul Elkins
(Based on stories by Bernice Mason and Sy Bartlett)
Starring: Lawrence Tibbett, Gregory Ratoff, Wendy
Barrie

1937 DANGER, LOVE AT WORK
Screenplay: James Edward Grant and Ben Markson
(Based on a story by James Edward Grant)
Starring: Ann Sothern, Jack Haley, Edward Everett
Horton

1943   MARGIN FOR ERROR
Screenplay: Lillie Hayward
(Based on a play by Clare Boothe Luce)
Starring: Joan Bennett, Milton Berle, Otto Preminger

1944   IN THE MEANTIME, DARLING
Screenplay: Arthur Kober and Michael Uris
Starring: Jeanne Crain, Frank Latimore, Mary Nash, Eugene Pallette

1944   LAURA
Screenplay: Jay Dratler, Samuel Hoffenstein, and Betty Reinhardt
(Based on a novel by Vera Caspary)
Starring: Gene Tierney, Dana Andrews, Clifton Webb, Vincent Price

1945   ROYAL SCANDAL (British title: CZARINA)
Screenplay: Edwin Justus Mayer
(Adapted by Bruno Frank from the play *The Czarina* by Lajos Biro and Melchior Lengyel)
Starring: Tallulah Bankhead, Charles Coburn, Anne Baxter, William Eythe

1945   FALLEN ANGEL
Screenplay: Harry Kleiner
(Based on a novel by Marty Holland)
Starring: Dana Andrews, Alice Faye, Linda Darnell, Charles Bickford

1946   CENTENNIAL SUMMER
Screenplay: Michael Kanin
(Based on the novel by Albert E. Idell)
Starring: Linda Darnell, Jeanne Crain, Cornel Wilde, William Eythe

1947   FOREVER AMBER
Screenplay: Philip Dunne and Ring Lardner, Jr.
(Adapted by Jerome Cady from the novel by Kathleen Windsor)
Starring: Linda Darnell, Cornel Wilde, Richard Greene, George Sanders

1947  DAISY KENYON
   Screenplay: David Hertz
   (Based on the novel by Elizabeth Janeway)
   Starring: Joan Crawford, Dana Andrews, Henry Fonda
1948  THAT LADY IN ERMINE
   Screenplay: Samson Raphaelson
   (Based on an operetta by Rudolph Schanzer and
   E. Welisch)
   Starring: Betty Grable, Douglas Fairbanks, Jr., Cesar
   Romero
1949  THE FAN (British title: LADY WINDERMERE'S FAN)
   Screenplay: Walter Reisch, Dorothy Parker, and Ross
   Evans
   (Based on the play *Lady Windermere's Fan* by Oscar
   Wilde)
   Starring: Jeanne Crain, Madeleine Carroll, George
   Sanders
1949  WHIRLPOOL
   Screenplay: Ben Hecht (under pseudonym Lester Bar-
   tow) and Andrew Solt
   (Based on the novel by Guy Endore)
   Starring: Gene Tierney, Richard Conte, Jose Ferrer
1950  WHERE THE SIDEWALK ENDS
   Screenplay: Rex Connor
   (Based on an adaptation by Victor Trivas, Frank P. Rosen-
   berg, and Robert E. Kent of a novel by William L. Stuart)
   Starring: Dana Andrews, Gene Tierney, Gary Merrill
1950  THE THIRTEENTH LETTER
   Screenplay: Howard Koch
   (Based on a script by Louis Chavance for *Le Corbeau*,
   H.-G. Clouzot, 1943)
   Starring: Linda Darnell, Charles Boyer, Michael Rennie
1952  ANGEL FACE
   Screenplay: Frank Nugent and Oscar Millard
   (Based on a story by Chester Erskine)
   Starring: Robert Mitchum, Jean Simmons

1953  THE MOON IS BLUE
Screenplay: F. Hugh Herbert
(Based on his play *The Moon Is Blue*)
Starring: William Holden, Maggie McNamara, David Niven

1954  RIVER OF NO RETURN
Screenplay: Frank Fenton
(Based on a story by Louis Lantz)
Starring: Robert Mitchum, Marilyn Monroe, Tommy Rettig

1954  CARMEN JONES
Screenplay: Harry Kleiner
(Based on a musical comedy by Oscar Hammerstein II)
Starring: Dorothy Dandridge, Harry Belafonte, Pearl Bailey, Diahann Carroll

1955  THE COURT-MARTIAL OF BILLY MITCHELL (British title: ONE MAN MUTINY)
Screenplay: Milton Sperling and Emmet Lavery
(Based on a true story by General William Mitchell)
Starring: Gary Cooper, Charles Bickford, Rod Steiger, Ralph Bellamy

1955  THE MAN WITH THE GOLDEN ARM
Screenplay: Walter Newman and Lewis Meltzer
(Based on the novel by Nelson Algren)
Starring: Frank Sinatra, Kim Novak, Eleanor Parker, Arnold Stang, Darren McGavin

1957  SAINT JOAN
Screenplay: Graham Greene
(Based on the play *Saint Joan* by George Bernard Shaw)
Starring: Jean Seberg, Richard Widmark, Richard Todd

1957  BONJOUR TRISTESSE
Screenplay: Arthur Laurents
(Based on the novel by Françoise Sagan)
Starring: David Niven, Deborah Kerr, Jean Seberg

1959  PORGY AND BESS
Screenplay: Richard Nash

(Based on the stage operetta by George Gershwin from the novel *Porgy* by DuBose and Dorothy Heyward)
Starring: Sidney Poitier, Dorothy Dandridge, Sammy Davis, Jr., Pearl Bailey

1959 ANATOMY OF A MURDER
Screenplay: Wendell Mayes
(Based on the novel by Robert Traver)
Starring: James Stewart, Lee Remick, Ben Gazzara, Joseph N. Welch

1960 EXODUS
Screenplay: Dalton Trumbo
(Based on the novel *Exodus* by Leon Uris)
Starring: Paul Newman, Eva Marie Saint, Ralph Richardson, Peter Lawford, Lee J. Cobb, Sal Mineo

1962 ADVISE AND CONSENT
Screenplay: Wendell Mayes
(Based on the novel *Advise and Consent* by Allen Drury)
Starring: Henry Fonda, Charles Laughton, Don Murray, Walter Pidgeon, Gene Tierney, Peter Lawford

1963 THE CARDINAL
Screenplay: Robert Dozier
(Based on the novel by Henry Morton Robinson)
Starring: Tom Tryon, Carol Lynley, John Huston, Raf Vallone

1964 IN HARM'S WAY
Screenplay: Wendell Mayes
(Based on the novel by James Bassett)
Starring: John Wayne, Kirk Douglas, Patricia Neal

1965 BUNNY LAKE IS MISSING
Screenplay: John and Penelope Mortimer
(Based on the novel by Evelyn Piper)
Starring: Keir Dullea, Carol Lynley, Laurence Olivier

1966 HURRY SUNDOWN
Screenplay: Thomas C. Ryan and Horton Foote
(Based on the novel by K. and B. Gilden)

Starring: Michael Caine, Jane Fonda, Faye Dunaway, John Phillip Law, Diahann Carroll, Robert Hooks

1968  SKIDOO

Original Screenplay: Doran William Cannon

Starring: Carol Channing, Jackie Gleason, Groucho Marx, John Phillip Law, Alexandra Hay

1970  TELL ME THAT YOU LOVE ME, JUNIE MOON

Screenplay: Marjorie Kellogg

(Based on her own novel)

Starring: Liza Minnelli, Ken Howard, Robert Moore, James Coco

1971  SUCH GOOD FRIENDS

Screenplay: Elaine May (under the pseudonym Esther Dale)

(Based on the novel by Lois Gould)

Starring: Dyan Cannon, James Coco, Jennifer O'Neill, Ken Howard

1975  ROSEBUD

Screenplay: Erik Lee Preminger

(Based on the novel by Paul Bonnecarrère and Joan Hemingway)

Starring: Peter O'Toole, Richard Attenborough, Cliff Gorman, Claude Dauphin, John V. Lindsay, Peter Lawford

# INDEX